In This Dark House

To Linda —

Thank you for a wonderful
evening. Walk box

Wishes, *[signature]*

603 835 5525

In This

Dark

House

A Memoir

∽

L o u i s e   K e h o e

SCHOCKEN BOOKS
NEW YORK

For Roman and Fenya

All rights reserved under International and Pan-American
Copyright Conventions. Published in the United States by
Schocken Books, a division of Random House, Inc., New York,
and simultaneously in Canada by Random House of Canada Limited,
Toronto. Distributed by Pantheon Books, a division of Random
House, Inc., New York. Originally published in hardcover by
Schocken Books, a division of Random House, Inc., 1995.

*Grateful acknowledgement is made to the following for permission to
reprint previously published material: The Estate of Edward Davison*:
"In This Dark House" from *Heart's Unreason* by Edward Davison,
copyright © 1940 by Edward Davison. Copyright renewed 1968 by
Edward Davison. Reprinted by permission of The Estate of Edward
Davison, Peter Davison, executor. • *Peters Fraser and Dunlop
Group Ltd.*: Excerpt from "Matilda" from *Cautionary Verses*
by Hilaire Belloc. Reprinted by permission of Peters Fraser
and Dunlop Group Ltd.

Library of Congress Cataloging-in-Publication Data
Kehoe, Louse, 1949-
In this dark house: a memoir / Louise Kehoe.
cm.
ISBN 0-8052-1017-2
1. Lubetkin, Berthold, 1901-1990. 2. Architects—England—
Biography. 3. Kehoe, Louise, 1949- —Family. I. Title.
NA997.L76K45 1995 720'.92—dc20 [B]

Printed in the United States of America
First Schocken Paperback Edition 2001
2 4 6 8 9 7 5 3 1

This book represents the truth as I see it, but because of the sheer complexity of the story it has been necessary to introduce occasional elements of fiction. In addition, the names of a number of individuals and places have been changed in order to protect certain individuals' privacy.

$\mathcal{P}$art $\mathcal{O}$ne

∾

World's
End

$\mathcal{C}$ h a p t e r

1

෧ In the southwest of England, where the river Severn ambles gently through the undulating Cotswold countryside, the scenery is timeless and unmistakably agricultural. The landscape is latticed with natural hedgerows — prickly and impenetrable thickets of sweetbrier and hazel, hawthorn and elder — which divide field from field and farm from farm along ancient boundaries. The narrow, winding roads are used by livestock more than by cars, and the few drivers who do negotiate those twists and turns do so at snail's pace, knowing that they may at any moment come upon a flock of sheep or a herd of cattle plodding sedately toward their barn at milking time.

The village of Upper Killington does not appear on any map. Indeed, despite its rather grandiose name, it can hardly be described as a village at all, nor even a hamlet. There are just three houses there; three seventeenth-century stone-built farmhouses nestling comfortably in the shelter of a little valley.

My parents discovered Upper Killington entirely by accident. It was 1939, just before the outbreak of the Second World War, and they had not long been married. They lived in London then, where my father's architectural practice was based, and were driving back to London after spending a weekend with friends in the west country when a particularly beautiful sunset made them want to stop for a while and just look. Leaving their car beside a ramshackle hay barn, they wandered down an anonymous-looking dirt road and suddenly found themselves in the little valley, its patient old houses suffused with the sunset's triumphant light. One of the three houses stood empty and abandoned, its garden waist-high in grass and weeds, its rough-hewn front door obscured by a heavy curtain of wisteria whose inquisitive tendrils had wormed their way through the keyhole and around the doorjamb, and could be seen advancing greedily across the flagstoned floor within.

To my parents, the pull of this beautiful backwater must have seemed irresistible. The country was on the brink of war; uncertainty permeated every aspect of daily life. Bomb shelters were hurriedly being constructed in towns and cities all over England, and propaganda posters had begun appearing everywhere. "Careless Talk Costs Lives," the posters proclaimed apocalyptically, warning people not to talk unguardedly to anyone: you never knew who might be listening, who might be a spy or a Nazi sympathizer. In this atmosphere of mounting dread and queasy instability Upper Killington, isolated and untouched by the troubles of the twentieth century, offered an oasis of immutable calm and reassuring predictability.

They returned to London but could not settle. Before the end of that year they had bought the empty house at Upper Killington and the hundred acres of farmland that went with it. Because of its blissful remoteness — but also, I suspect, because of the catastrophe which was about to engulf Europe — they called the house World's End.

$\mathcal{C}$ h a p t e r

2

⚬⚬ The dirt road leading to Upper Killington was knee-deep in mud when my parents moved into World's End in the winter of 1939, and the moving van could not get down to the valley. Instead, it had to be unloaded at the top of the hill and the contents ferried laboriously to the house on a tractor and trailer driven by one of the local farmers, a mountain of a man by the name of Alf Chapel.

This was only the first of Alf's many kindnesses. Alf knew every inch of Upper Killington like the back of his hand: he had been born in the very house in which he was now raising a family of his own, and his father and grandfather had farmed the same land before him. It was extremely rare in those days for ownership of a farm to change other than by family succession, and talk about the newcomers at Upper Killington had long preceded their rather undignified arrival. Alf had heard his fair share of rumors and speculation; sitting around the fire in the pub with the other local farmers he had listened as they gossiped, their stories growing taller and taller under the influence of the landlord's stupefyingly strong home-brewed cider. But Alf had a level head and a generous heart, and although he was as curious as any as to why a Russian architect and his young wife would want to move to a derelict farm in the heart of rural England, his inclination was to wait and see.

He didn't have long to wait. Talking to my parents as they sat amid the sea of tea chests and cardboard boxes in the empty farmhouse, it rapidly became clear to him that they had bought World's End on a whim, and that although they were obviously infatuated with the idea of becoming farmers, they knew next to nothing about what was involved. He decided to take them under his wing; and that was just as well, for if he hadn't, my parents, armed as they were with nothing but the blind enthusiasm of the amateur and a twelve-volume encyclopedia of veterinary science, would surely soon have found themselves hopelessly out of their depth.

The local farmers were not the only ones to wonder what on earth could have possessed my parents to make them embark on this venture. When my father announced to his partners that his days as an architect were over, and that he and my mother intended to move to Upper Killington without delay and become farmers, they reacted with a mixture of consternation and incredulity. After all, my father, Berthold Lubetkin, then not quite forty, was at the pinnacle of his career, and the avant-garde architectural practice which he had founded shortly after his arrival in England in 1930 had become the talk of London's artistic and intellectual circles. His colleagues knew him as a man seemingly totally committed to his chosen profession, a passionate idealist and inspired designer whose uncompromising perfectionism, exasperating though it could be, always managed to bring out the very best in those who worked alongside him. And now here he was, on the point of leaving architecture as abruptly as he had arrived, and talking with enormous enthusiasm about becoming a farmer.

But discontent was in his nature: regardless of how much success and acclaim he won for his work, it never seemed to satisfy him for long. The meandering path which had brought him to England bore witness to the restlessness of his spirit. He had gone from the wealth and comfort of his childhood in imperial Russia to an impoverished, bohemian studenthood in Warsaw, Paris and Berlin; he had known the anonymity and bewilderment of the newly arrived immigrant, struggling to gain a toehold in an unfamiliar culture; he had mastered five languages, and had learned to bend them to his wit and his will like a native. His intellectual capacity was prodigious: he hungered for new places, new challenges, conquered them quickly and longed to move on.

That same restlessness had been evident in his behavior toward women, and he had earned himself a reputation as something of a philanderer. Handsome, cosmopolitan and brilliantly funny, women were naturally drawn to him, and he to them — but he shunned commitment like the plague. My mother, Margaret Church, was only nineteen when she met him. She was then a student at England's most prestigious architectural school, and she had gone to an interview for a summer job at my father's practice. Her youth and beauty elicited a predictable reaction from my father, who set his sights on her at once. She never stood a chance.

She was the youngest of three girls born into a wealthy English family. Her father had been killed in the First World War, while she was still only a baby, and she had no memory of him. Nevertheless, she felt the lack of a father keenly, and grew up revering him: all her life she kept a faded photograph of him in his army uniform, and it was precious to her. Tucked into one corner of the battered antique silver frame there was a tiny photograph of his gravestone — one of thousands upon thousands of identical white marble monuments marching forever in step across the haunted, windswept fields of northern France. With a magnifying glass one could just make out the inscription on the headstone: "Captain Harold Church, Oxon & Bucks Light Infantry. Somme, July 1st, 1916," and then the epitaph: "Onward, Christian Soldier." Such was her pride in her dead father that as a child she was unshakably convinced that the Lord's Prayer opened with the words "Our Father, who art in Heaven, Harold be Thy Name." It had come as both a shock and a disappointment to her when, having learned to read, she discovered that the official version was addressed to someone else entirely.

My father, almost twice her age, so accomplished, so handsome and so mesmerizingly strong-willed, must have seemed to her the personification of the father she had never had, and her devotion to him was immediate, unwavering and lifelong. She deferred to him in all things, believing his to be the better mind and the sounder judgment, even when her intuition, her conscience and her abundant common sense told her otherwise. When he encouraged her to give up her studies and come to work for him she hardly thought twice, even though her place at architectural school had been hard-won. (She had been the youngest student ever to be admitted there, and one of the very first women.) And when he invited her to leave the London flat she shared with her sisters and move in with him, she did so without a second's hesitation.

For the next four years they defied convention by living as man and wife when they were nothing of the sort, an arrangement that scandalized her mother, who, herself the very soul of propriety, was horrified that her daughter could see fit to jeopardize the good name of the family by living in sin — and to make matters worse, the man was a foreigner. She must have lived in dread of the announcement of a pregnancy — but she needn't have worried: in this matter, at least, she and my father were entirely in accord, although for vastly different reasons. My father's fear of parenthood had nothing whatever to do with questions of legitimacy or decorum: he simply did not want to be tied down. For despite his sincere and unprecedentedly deep feelings for my mother, he remained restive and rootless at heart; a baby would impede his mobility, restrict his choices and impose its needs on him; becoming a father would be profoundly inconvenient.

But birth control in those days was unreliable at best, and while my mother did what she could to dodge pregnancy, it seemed as though fate had cast her ineluctably as a mother. During the four years of their unofficial marriage she became pregnant several times, and although she wanted very much to have the babies, my father insisted categorically on her getting rid of them. Abortions back then were illegal, extremely difficult to obtain and terrifyingly unsafe, but my father was adamant, and my mother, scared stiff of losing the man she loved so much, obediently ended each of her pregnancies under circumstances which, for the rest of her life, she remained deeply reluctant to discuss.

By 1939, perhaps stampeded by the general nervousness which pervaded those ominous months before war broke out, and maybe influenced, also, by the desirability of acquiring British nationality and the right to reside permanently in England, my father decided he was at last ready to make a formal commitment to my mother. Since they were both atheists, they shunned a traditional wedding, choosing instead to solemnize their marriage in a strictly secular ceremony. On a stubbornly rainy late spring day they entered the registrar's office at Chelsea Town Hall, emerging as man and wife not many minutes later, to walk a gauntlet of their friends and architectural colleagues, each of whom held a T square aloft in a parody of the crossed swords of a military guard of honor.

If it was architecture that had brought my parents together, politics was undoubtedly the cement which united them, for both had come of age in a time of tremendous social and political instability, a time when it was as impossible to ignore the inequities of the old order as it was to remain indifferent to the challenges posed by the new.

My father was born in czarist Russia in 1901, the child of wealthy parents who had homes in Moscow and St. Petersburg. He grew up surrounded by the gilded opulence and bejeweled excess of the dying years of the Romanov empire, and like many of his generation who had witnessed at first hand the decadence and savage cruelty of the imperial regime, he turned to communism, rejoicing in the revolution of 1917, and embracing the doctrines of Marx and Lenin as though they held the key to all the mysteries of the universe. He professed himself a communist for the rest of his life, never allowing a word of criticism for the Soviet Union to pass his lips — although since he had been shrewd enough to remove himself from the epicenter of the Bolshevik earthquake and its even more deadly Stalinist aftershocks by settling in England, his fidelity to the ideology of communism was never as sorely tested as it undoubtedly would have been had he stayed in the country of his birth.

My mother's political awakening took a rather gentler path. She, too, was born into wealth; her family were heirs to a fortune amassed by her grandfather, a sour and humorless man whose affluence was belied by his sweeping and obsessive stinginess. His miserliness made a deep impression on her, even as a little girl, and in later life she would recall how, when visiting his London club, he would remove his luxurious astrakhan coat before entering the building, and hand it to his chauffeur with instructions to deposit it with the pawnbroker around the corner. This he did because the coat could be retrieved the same day from the pawnbroker without costing him a penny, whereas if he had handed it in at the club's cloakroom he would have been obliged to tip the attendant.

My mother's suffocatingly respectable English education was buttressed on all sides by the Church of England, and her schooling was fortified with generous doses of biblical and Christian instruction, much of which stayed with her for the rest of her life — though surely not at all in the way her teachers had intended.

Each Sunday her entire family, with all their servants, attended a small country church near their home. As the service drew to an end, the vicar would conclude his prayers with the benediction *God bless the squire and his relations, and keep us in our proper stations.*

Something about this pious supplication troubled her. She had already incurred her mother's strong disapproval for fraternizing with the servants and spending time with them in the cavernous kitchen belowstairs. "Servants," her mother had admonished her, "are not like us; people from the lower classes cannot think or feel as we do. They are born to serve as we are born to lead, and they are perfectly content with their lot." But despite her mother's assurances that the status quo was eminently satisfactory to both parties, my mother remained quietly unhappy about the way life seemed to be organized, and continued to befriend the servants, listening to their conversations and learning about their lives, their hardships, their hopes and their fears.

The parlormaid had a little boy my mother's age, and on Sunday afternoons he would come to the back door of the kitchen, where his mother would meet him and furtively hand him his weekly treat: a slab of bread spread thickly with the drippings from the pan in which the Sunday roast had been cooked for the lady of the house and her three daughters. One day my mother asked the little boy why he wore no shoes; it was winter, and his feet were blue with cold. "Ain't got no shoes," the child replied, blushing with shame and humiliation. It was then that my mother's misgivings began to harden into something resembling indignation, and she gave her mother no peace until she agreed to buy the parlormaid's son a pair of new shoes.

When her grandfather died, my mother boldly challenged her family's serenely confident assertion that the parsimonious old man was now safely installed in Heaven, and cited no lesser source than the Bible to back up her argument. "He can't be in Heaven," she protested. "The Bible says that it's easier for a camel to pass through the eye of a needle than for a rich man to enter the gates of Heaven."

The whole concept of wealth made her distinctly uneasy. She found it impossible to reconcile her family's comfort and prosperity with the obvious poverty of those to whom her mother referred as "the lower classes." She was a child during the 1920s, a period of massive unemployment and hardship in England, when long lines of ragged, downcast people were to be seen shuffling in numb despondency toward soup kitchens in towns and cities across the land. The images of these hopeless, hungry people haunted her, filling her with outrage. She became a communist in her heart long before she had ever heard of Marx or Engels, and although she very quickly learned to dress her burgeoning social conscience in the drab and leaden language of dialectical materialism, she never lost the anger and the passion that had first goaded her into political awareness.

Now, newly married and faced with the farm at World's End to run, my parents found confidence and courage in the political philosophy they shared. For though they knew almost nothing about agriculture, they viewed farming as fundamentally dignified, ennobling work, and farmers such as their guardian angel Alf Chapel as the salt of the earth, the very bedrock of socialism.

My father, who at the outbreak of the war was too old to be drafted, had instead enlisted in the only army open to him: the Land Army. The Land Army, despite its military-sounding name, was actually an exclusively civilian organization, run by the government Ministry of Agriculture in association with British farmers, the purpose of which was to ensure the supply of food to the beleaguered nation during wartime. The entire output of the farm therefore was committed to the war effort, an arrangement which fueled my parents' sense of purpose and added to their determination to rehabilitate the neglected land. For their part, the Ministry of Agriculture supplied a steady stream of pale academics and theoreticians whose mission it was to exorcise the folklore from farming and to sow in its place a reverence for the newer, scientific approach. This, of course, met with an enthusiastic reception from my parents, ardent

disciples that they were of Five-Year Plans and collec-
tivization; but the likes of Alf, who had been successfully
coaxing forth crops and livestock from this land for genera-
tions, listened in polite silence to the missionaries from the
Ministry of Agriculture, and continued to farm precisely as
they always had, fertilizing their fields with manure instead of commercial superphosphate, and allowing their
cows to decide the place and time of their own calving, in
barefaced defiance of Ministry orders.

On this diet of idealism, textbook agronomy and Alf
Chapel's bottomless generosity, the farm soon regained its
composure and began to flourish. Of course, there was
plenty of encouragement from friends, too. World's End in
those days was a magnet for the many intellectuals and
artists of my parents' London circle who shared their vision
of a socialist utopia, and for whom a few days spent in
strenuous physical work on the farm came about as close to
a spiritual experience as was possible within the sober
doctrinal confines of their uniformly devout atheism. In the
evenings they would sit around the old refectory table in
the low-ceilinged kitchen, chain-smoking and talking ani-
matedly, their faces a spectral yellow in the kerosene
lamp's hissing, conspiratorial light.

Always, talk was of the war; of the destruction being
wrought on London and other English cities by Hitler's in-
discriminate bombing; of the growing possibility of a Nazi
invasion of England — and of what would become of people such as themselves if such an invasion were to take
place. For Hitler's loathing of communism was legendary,
and exceeded only by his loathing of Jews. Indeed, in the

tortuous and haunted corridors of the Nazi mind the two were inextricably connected: communism was perceived as the brainchild of the Jews, a nefarious Zionist plot to gain control of the whole world. It was Hitler's avowed intention to crush the Soviet Union, just as it was his avowed intention to annihilate European Jewry — and by the summer of 1942 it was beginning to look as though he might succeed in doing both.

As the news from the war front grew steadily more alarming, my parents found a measure of consolation in immersing themselves in the practicalities of running the farm. Planting, harvesting and animal husbandry have reassuring rhythms and imperatives of their own, and by focusing their attention on the daily demands of farming they were able to maintain the illusion of control, stability and permanence. The quiet valley, where miniature daffodils grew wild in exuberant clumps among the gnarled old apple trees, and skylarks circled and chattered above the rustling cornfields, was a world removed from imperial St. Petersburg, but for the first time in his life my father felt truly at home.

Several photographs and sketches by visiting artist friends still exist, vividly evoking the paradoxical happiness of those early years at World's End, when, confronted by absolute uncertainty, caution seemed pointless and the notion of risk no longer had any meaning. There are pictures of my mother carrying buckets to the barn, throwing grain to the chickens; drawings of my father driving a tractor across the hayfields; but the most poignant of them all is a painting of my mother, titled "Young Communist." A few simple brushstrokes have captured the essence of her inextinguishable hope for a better future. There she stands, dressed in a Ukrainian peasant's collarless, embroidered shirt, her gray-green eyes staring steadily ahead, full of earnestness and quiet conviction. She is cradling a baby in her arms: her firstborn, my sister, Sasha.

$\mathcal{C}$ h a p t e r

3

◌◌ I've often wondered at what point my father stopped calling my mother Maggie and instead began calling her Mama, which is the way Russian children address their mothers. Did my mother revel in her new name, seeing it as a sign that my father had at last accepted the idea of becoming a parent, that he had maybe even developed a shy enthusiasm for it? Did she practice using her new name as her pregnancy progressed, saying it quietly to herself, feeling its awkwardness, its strange power? Or was it just a habit she and my father fell into later on, perhaps prompted by their baby's first garbled attempts at speech? Whatever the precise chronology, the name change was absolute: my mother was Mama for the rest of her life, and her children never knew her or thought of her as anything else.

My father, on the other hand, could not be so easily summed up in a single paternal nickname. Mama always addressed him as "Darling" — and meant it — but when she spoke about him to us, she called him Dad. As far as we were concerned, though, "Dad" wasn't always adequate, for he rarely remained the same person for long; and while he could be eminently Dad-ish, or even Daddy-ish, one minute, he could turn as tyrannical and overbearing as the very worst sort of Victorian patriarch the next, and at those times "sir" would have suited him better. So although we called him Dad to his face, we often had cause to think of him in less endearing terms, and amongst ourselves, in whispered commiseration at the height of one of his storms, or in the bitterness of its aftermath, we found some small consolation in referring caustically to him as "The Führer."

My sister, Sasha, once told me that she believed the only reason she was born at all was because abortions were impossible to obtain during the war, and I think she may well have been right. The truth is, my parents would probably have been a great deal happier if they had never had children. Certainly Dad would have preferred it that way, as his unyielding insistence on Mama aborting all her previous pregnancies had amply demonstrated. Sixteen years her senior, he would have been perfectly happy to have drifted, unfettered, into a childless old age, remaining the sole object of her affection. Instead, he found himself compelled to share her with us, and this at a time of life when his reserves of equanimity and forbearance, never abundant to start with, had dwindled to an extent that virtually guaranteed conflict.

The antipathy which he had long felt toward fatherhood never really dissipated; if anything, it grew keener with the birth of each successive child. Oh, he liked us well enough when we were just little bundles waddling inelegantly along

like penguins, when we were still at the stage of mute and
unquestioning dependence; but once our nascent identities
began to emerge and we started to assert ourselves as individuals, his attitude changed dramatically. He ceased to re-
gard us as animated toys, whimsical objects, and began
instead to see us as habitual insubordinates, self-indulgent
little dilettantes whose characters — whose very thought
processes, even — it was his bounden duty to shape and
control with the utmost rigor.

Inevitably this put Mama at odds with him, for she not
only loved children (and would have had more, if only he
had allowed her to) but also she took active pride in her
children's quirks and individuality, and felt no desire at all
to constrain their burgeoning identities. However, stronger
even than her love for us was her absolute devotion to Dad,
and while we were certainly the source of much happiness
to her, we were undeniably also the source of a great deal of
contention between her and Dad. In this painful tug-of-war,
Dad's pull almost always prevailed, and it was his hand,
therefore, which gripped the reins, set the pace and steered
the course of our upbringing, while to Mama fell the unen-
viable job of go-between, cajoling us into compliance with
his often glaringly unreasonable directives and defending
his decisions, no matter how punitive and unfair they were.

For our part, shrewdly detecting our mother's secret discomfort in this role, we looked to her as both a friend and
an intercessor, and by doing so, of course, we placed an
unbearable strain on her loyalties. But although we railed
bitterly against the injustices that Dad meted out to us with
her complicity, we loved her no less — and maybe even

loved her more — because we sensed her predicament and her dilemma. Besides, we knew beyond doubt that she loved us dearly.

No such certainty blessed our relationship with Dad. His love was capricious, brazenly conditional and in permanently short supply. If one of us was temporarily able to bask in the coveted warmth of his approbation it was only because the other two had been pushed unceremoniously out into the cold. He constantly compared and criticized us. If one of us had earned praise or congratulations, he never missed the opportunity to disparage the others, and to point out the many ways in which they had fallen short of his expectations and disappointed him. From our earliest youth he deliberately set us against one another, the better to control us, using our natural hunger for his affection as a tool with which to widen and deepen our individual differences, and igniting a savage rivalry among us, a hawk-eyed and unsleeping jealousy which smoldered on unabated long after we were fledged and flown.

Life in the Lubetkin family was a perpetual shell game. Dad manipulated the shells with all the unscrupulousness and cunning of a hustler, and we, hopelessly addicted to the vision of winning his love, learned to fight ferociously with the world and with one another, never allowing ourselves for a moment to consider the painful possibility that the shells had always been empty, and always would be.

It is said that children come into the world with their minds a blank slate — a tabula rasa, the experts call it, clothing the concept in Latin and thereby bestowing upon it an aura of solemn and unimpeachable scientific verity. And indeed it may well be so; but however blank their minds, I believe children are born with a sort of psychic map and compass (the Latin for which, I am ashamed to admit, I do not know), and what they lack in abstract reasoning ability they more than make up for in powers of divination. Far from hindering their ability to make sense of the world around them, the absence of intellectual baggage actually lends them a certain freedom of mobility and allows them to lean with absolute confidence on their own intuition. Children are particularly astute when it comes to sensing the unspoken messages and hidden agendas which are subtly woven into their parents' behavior, and Sasha was no exception to this rule. Her map and compass served her well, detecting very early and with extraordinary accuracy the deep fault lines that ran through our family.

She was a beautiful child; her black hair and dark eyes were an emphatic reminder of Dad's Russian origins, and contrasted strikingly with Mama's fair-skinned Englishness. For the first three years of her life, she wallowed happily in the concentrated doting which is the peculiar privilege of the firstborn: she was universally admired, incessantly photographed and her every move and murmur faithfully chronicled in a voluminous baby journal. This suited her well, for she was a born actress; she had a love for the limelight and an almost visceral need to be the center of attention.

In the summer of 1945, just as the war finally came to an end, a second child, Andrew, was born. Inevitably,

Andrew's arrival brought an end to Sasha's ascendancy; like any firstborn, she suffered agonies of resentment over her parents' sudden besottedness with the newcomer. But hers was no transient surge of sibling rivalry. Goaded by a growing awareness that Dad's love was frighteningly inconstant and subject to sudden and inexplicable withdrawal, she turned the full force of her jealous rage on Andrew, hating him with a persistence and intensity that neither time nor the birth of a third child, Steven, could assuage.

Andrew was as fair as Sasha was dark, and as tranquil as she was vivacious: he was in every way her opposite, and this only heightened her hatred of him, for she could not hope to emulate those qualities of his which were lacking in herself, and to which her parents were so fond of drawing attention. She tormented him at every opportunity, taking a particular pleasure in tiptoeing to his cot as he slept and pinching his soft flesh as hard as she could — a torture for which she even devised a special name: "pweeging." But poor Andrew's sufferings were not solely of Sasha's making. He was a sickly child, succumbing to ear and throat infections with monotonous regularity. After the third such bout in the space of a few months, a tonsillectomy was strongly recommended by the family physician. Shortly before his fourth birthday, Andrew was admitted to the same small country hospital in which he had been born. With promises of endless ice cream when he awoke, Mama kissed her little son and bade him good night, sleep tight. He was wheeled, peacefully anesthetized, into the operating room, where the surgeon, a generalist more accustomed to suturing cuts and tears for hefty farmhands than to the delicate dissection involved in throat surgery on such a miniature patient, botched the procedure and accidentally severed the child's jugular vein. Andrew died within seconds, drowning in his own blood.

Steven, still only a baby, neither knew who Andrew was nor noticed his absence; but Sasha, then seven, fully understood the extent of the disaster which had befallen the family, and moreover she felt in no small way responsible for it. Hadn't she, after all, almost daily wished Andrew dead? Hadn't she dreamed of the day when she would be free of her detested rival? But instead of unbridled happiness, Sasha felt a terrible sense of guilt; and instead of enabling her to recapture her parents' undivided attention, Andrew's death seemed somehow to have put them entirely beyond her reach. For almost at once, a thick curtain of silence was pulled around the entire subject of Andrew; the circumstances of his death were never explained to her; photographs of him disappeared without trace, and his name was never mentioned again. Indeed, it was not until she was eighteen that she finally found out what had happened that terrible day — and even then it was not Mama or Dad who told her, but an aunt.

Acutely aware of the taboo surrounding Andrew, Sasha could not turn to Mama and Dad for reassurance and exoneration. Besides, she knew in her heart that she had behaved despicably toward Andrew, and if she confessed to them how much she had hated him, how she had pweeged him and punished him simply for having been born, they would surely hate her in turn. She therefore had nowhere

to go with her guilt; she could not escape from the knowledge that she had willed her brother's death, that she had
actively wanted the very thing that had now brought such
profound grief to her parents. She had never needed their
love more, nor felt less deserving of it. The choices were
clear to her: if she broke the taboo and bared her soul to
Mama and Dad, she stood to lose everything. If she col-
luded with them in their silence she would keep their love
— but only, she was sure, because they were ignorant of
how utterly unworthy of that love she was. She chose to
stay silent: better to be loved on false pretenses than not to
be loved at all.

This compromise cost Sasha dearly. The burden of guilt
lay heavily on her, and she was left with an indelible conviction of her own inner ugliness — a conviction she strove
to counter by seeking praise and approval from outside
sources. Her need for others to think well of her amounted
to outright dependence; she needed a constant supply of
admiration, and if admiration was not forthcoming, then
mere attention would do — anything rather than anonymity; she hated to be alone. Her natural tendency toward ex-
hibitionism now became a cornerstone of her character: she
was never happier than when she had an audience. People
sustained her: from them she got what she could not provide
for herself; she hungered for their applause and dreaded
their indifference. Even her childish drawings reflected her
overwhelming need to stand out, to be admired. The themes
were single-mindedly theatrical: an actress or ballerina
being showered with bouquets; a sparkling, bewitching solo
performer responding to the adulation of the crowd.

But the more expert she became in eliciting the approval she craved from others, the less it satisfied her, and the more undeserving of it she felt. She was haunted by the thought that if people really knew who she was, knew how she had behaved to Andrew and what jealous hatred she had harbored toward him, they would shun her instead of admiring her. She began to feel like a fraud, an impostor, and this only added to the bitter sense of unworthiness that was now her constant companion. She could never be confident in her friendships, for she felt they were founded on falsity, and her fear of being exposed as the shallow and unlovable person she felt herself to be caused her agonies of insecurity. This tangle of unresolved feelings inevitably tightened into a knot of such unyielding complexity that it became a permanent feature of her psychological landscape.

Sasha was almost eight when I was born, and by then she was too deeply involved in the social life and activities of her school to view my coming as any sort of threat. She told me she thought of me more as an animated doll than as a potential rival for the affections of Mama and Dad, and she never felt the need to pweeg me as I slept. But the ghost of Andrew was not to be so easily laid.

I was still very young when she told me about my dead brother; about how beautiful he was, and how much loved, and about how he had gone into the hospital and never come back. I may have been young, but my map and compass served me well: I understood instinctively that I must never, under any circumstances, mention Andrew's name to Mama or Dad, or ask about his death. I understood, too, and with a devastating clarity, Sasha's assertion that I would never have been born at all but for Andrew's untimely death, and that consequently I was and never would be anything other than second best, a poor replacement, a mere makeweight.

The seeds of self-doubt germinate easily in such sad soil, and flourish in such desolate climates. While part of me burned with determination to prove to my parents that I was every inch my dead brother's equal, to earn their love and erase the pain that Andrew's death had caused them, there was another part: a whining, leaden, hopeless part that expounded, at length and without pity, on the futility of even trying — and my childhood became a secret battleground between the two.

Mama and Dad found it endearingly funny when, at the age of just four, I solemnly announced that I had composed a song for them, and then, after plaintively singing the one and only line — "If you want me to, I will" — I dissolved into floods of tears. They never for a moment suspected the passion which had inspired the composition, nor the deep and ineffable sadness that brought the performance so abruptly to an end.

$\mathcal{C}$ h a p t e r
4

෴ It took a certain amount of determination to find World's End. Road signs weren't the slightest use: they petered out miles away, denying all knowledge of Upper Killington and its whereabouts, and if you hadn't been warned to look out for a dilapidated old hay barn standing all alone at an insignificant-looking crossroads, you would almost certainly have missed the turning and driven right past the only road that led there. The crossroads was known locally as Starvenhall, and it used to mystify me that such a godforsaken spot should have been dignified with its own name at all. Many years later I discovered that the name Starvenhall meant "the place where all will freeze" in the ancient dialect of rural southwest England, and that made eminently good sense to me, for the crossroads stood at the crest of a hill and was exposed in every direction, and the road that led down the hill into the valley ran full into the face of the east wind as it roared up from the Bristol Channel. Cold it was, and memorably so.

I was almost ten years old when power lines finally found their way to Upper Killington. Before that there was no electricity at World's End; the house was lit with kerosene lamps and heating was something we just did without. There were fireplaces in several of the rooms, but they were seldom graced with fire: my parents prized them as original architectural features, and treated them with a reverence which precluded their use as real grates in anything but the most exceptional circumstances — and mere cold weather did not qualify. The house had thick stone walls and flag-stoned floors, and although it faced southwest the fickle English sun could never do more than lend its gentle golden light to the exterior; inside, the house remained sepul-chrally cold. Chilblains would appear on my toes with the first frosts of autumn, and would stay there, itching and throbbing and angrily demanding more shoe-room until the daffodils emerged to trumpet the coming of spring.

The only warm room in the house was the kitchen, where an old-fashioned cast-iron coal stove provided back-ground warmth and heat for cooking. Above the stove there hung a laundry rack, suspended on a system of pulleys. Each morning Mama would lower the rack and load it with the clothes she had painstakingly washed and wrung out by hand (there being no washing machine, of course). By lunchtime the low-ceilinged kitchen would be full of steam, and the clothes would be imbued with the flowery scent of parsley, thyme and bay leaves from the volumi-nous stockpot which ruminated night and day at the back of the stove.

The kitchen was dominated by an enormous rough-hewn table, at least twelve feet long and eight inches thick, which had been a refectory table in an orphanage. It still bore the carved initials of some of the small paupers who had once received their zealously overcooked institutional meals on its dark, uneven surface. At one end of the table there was a battery-powered radio, a large and uncompromisingly functional wooden box, through the perforated back panel of which a child's eye could pick out the glowing vacuum tubes, and watch the interleaving parallel plates of the condenser which moved so satisfyingly apart and together at the bidding of the tuning knob. In the years since the war my parents had become progressively more reclusive, allowing many of their old friendships to wither slowly away through neglect. Every year fewer Christmas cards arrived, and fewer still were sent. World's End rarely saw visitors anymore, and if it had not been for my daily attendance at school, I might have had no contact at all with the outside world other than that brought to me by the BBC, in the Queen's most pedantically enunciated English, over that radio.

Quite why my parents had chosen to withdraw from the world in this way it never occurred to me to ask; it was simply a fact of life. The hermetic isolation of Upper Killington was the only thing I had ever known — I was born there, after all — and besides, I had no memory of my parents as the gregarious people they had reputedly been when they first met. As far as I was concerned, they had always been militantly antisocial. When people did visit, they were not encouraged to stay for long — I cannot recall there ever being an overnight guest at World's End — and after they had gone my parents would express enormous relief at the lifting of what they saw as a painful intrusion. There would follow a lengthy and detailed postmortem, during which they would subject their erstwhile visitors to minute and scathing criticism, dissecting their conversation, their opinions and even their table manners without pity, something I found enormously disconcerting in view of the apparent cordiality with which the fleeting guests had been received.

A child raised in an atmosphere of such resolute misanthropy cannot fail to be affected by it, and even before I reached school age I had begun to entertain the uneasy suspicion that my family was somehow different from other families, and that, for reasons I could neither understand nor articulate, I was destined to be an outsider.

School did little to dispel my misgivings. For a start, sheer distance put a well-nigh insurmountable barrier between me and my peers. The bus that took me to school and back — an hour's ride in each direction — left from the village of Hawkesworth, itself a half-hour ride by car from Upper Killington. My parents found the trip to Hawkesworth and back twice daily tiresome enough, and were unyielding in their opposition to my taking part in any after-school activities, for this would of necessity involve them in extra fetching and carrying. It was therefore rare indeed for me to go to the home of a classmate or to experience a taste of life outside the quarantined existence at World's End — and when I did, it only served to confirm my belief that the Lubetkin family was like no other, and that I was a misfit through and through.

But more than simply mileage stood between me and comfortable assimilation at school. Far from being separate, church and state in England were deeply and inextricably enmeshed with each other: all the schools were to a greater or lesser extent parochial, and prayer and religious education were an integral part of the curriculum. My parents, both avowed atheists, objected vehemently to my participation in any religious activity, and demanded that I pursue purely academic study during the periods when the rest of the school attended to devotional matters. This set me apart at once from every other child in the school, branding me indelibly in the eyes of pupils and staff alike. I dread to think what would have happened if I had been rash enough to reveal to my parents that the academic study arranged by the school for me as an alternative to religious education consisted of my sitting in an empty classroom, rote-learning the Psalms in numerical order and reciting them from memory in front of the entire class at the end of the study period. It is an irony which I am sure would not have been lost on my teachers that I can, to this day, summon up whole chunks of the lyrical hymns of King David, while remembering little or nothing about my other studies.

There was no escape, either, from the consequences of my parents' passionate political convictions. Contemptuously dismissing the mounting evidence of Stalin's monstrous crimes as nothing more than vicious anti-Soviet propaganda, Dad clung doggedly to his communist faith, while Mama echoed his pronouncements as though they had come down from the mountain carved on tablets of stone. Like a loyal commissar Dad stood guard over me, jealously policing my contact with the outside world and taking it upon himself to protect me from influences which he considered undesirable. Every day, as he drove me along the narrow, winding road to Hawkesworth to catch the school bus, he would take advantage of the time we had together to catechize me on current affairs, the car accelerating sharply with every forceful point he made, and meandering alarmingly while its driver's attention was wholly occupied elsewhere. As we neared Hawkesworth, he would sum up the lesson of the vertiginous journey with this homily, identical every day: *Now we are approaching the last and most dangerous corner, and the time at my disposal is strictly speaking limited. Nevertheless, before I release you to the school there is still time for me to express the fervent hope that when I return to fetch you this evening you will have become a worthier citizen than you are now.*

Many was the time I landed myself in hot water at school by regurgitating some wildly irreverent remark or transparently doctrinaire statement of Dad's. I was summoned by the headmistress of my junior school and made to apologize publicly, before the entire school, for blaspheming, after I made the mistake of referring to the Holy Ghost the way Dad did, as the Holy Goat. And I have never forgotten the explosive silence that descended on the classroom — a classroom packed with the children of dairy farmers — when I, eight years old and terrifyingly truthful, answered a teacher's question about the dietary value of milk by solemnly denouncing that paragon of health and natural purity, declaring it carcinogenic on account of the dangerously high strontium 90 levels which were present in it as a direct result of fallout from the testing of nuclear weapons in the atmosphere.

I was on no less perilous ground at home. After picking me up from the school bus at Hawkesworth in the evening, Dad would put me through what amounted to a full debriefing on the way home, demanding to know what I had learned that day — particularly in history classes — and would savagely dismember the information I dutifully relayed to him, condemning it as bourgeois revisionism and drumming his own — Marxist — interpretation mercilessly into me. The dilemma induced by these conflicting forces was agonizing: if I defended the version supplied by my teachers I would incur Dad's most withering scorn and anger, whereas if I expounded on Dad's ideas to my teachers they responded with crushing rebukes and punitive grading. Homework to which Dad had given the seal of doctrinal approval would regularly come back to me run through with an angry cat-scratch of red ink, the page puckered by the vehemence of the pen stroke. "I'm not interested in your pet theories; I asked for the FACTS!" wrote my furious history teacher on one memorable occasion. But to Dad these were the words of an idiot. He never tired of telling me, then and later on in my life, that the very notion of fact was itself a fantasy, particularly where history was concerned. "Facts," he said, "do not exist. The data one chooses to select and record depend solely upon the theory one is trying to prove. Facts are purely a matter of opinion."

Little did I realize, as I wrestled, exasperated, with the

seemingly insoluble problem of how to do my history homework to the satisfaction of both my judges, that Dad's disdain for facts was not the product of some lofty philosophical purism, nor even of simple sophistry, but came instead from the desperate desire he felt to escape from the awful realities of his own sad past.

C hapter

5

○◌ World's End was not a large house. Of the three
houses at Upper Killington, it was actually the smallest,
and would have fit almost twice over into the enormous
barn that stood behind and to one side of it. Both house
and barn were built of limestone, the most plentiful and
obliging material to be found in those parts at the latter
end of the seventeenth century, when they were commis-
sioned. The roof of the house was still clad in its original
limestone tiles, now so encrusted with mosses and lichens
that from the outside it was almost impossible to distin-
guish one tile from the next; but from the underside, as one
crawled along the rafters in the cramped and cobwebby
attic, the tiles appeared much as they must have done
when they were set there, each one pegged carefully in
place with a hand-whittled dowel. The roof of the barn,
however, had collapsed some years before the arrival of the
Lubetkins, and had been replaced with gray Welsh slate
— beautiful, to be sure, and a perfect foil for the warm,

golden limestone of the walls, but no self-respecting moss or lichen would think of taking up residence on its sleek, nonporous surface. It was a source of wry amusement to my architect parents that the modern roof of the barn was given to leaking quite brazenly when it rained, while the ancient moss-clad tiles above our heads took the worst of the English weather calmly in their stride, never allowing a single drop to penetrate their venerable defenses.

In one corner of the barn there stood a huge wooden cider press, almost two stories tall and sinister in the extreme to my young eye, not just for its sheer size, but also for its resemblance to some fiendish medieval instrument of torture. The press was certainly the largest for miles around, and according to local legend it was also unrivaled for the quality of cider it produced. Once a year, in late September, farmers from far and wide would arrive, their trailers piled high with apples to be pressed, and would leave with their wooden barrels full of the turbid extract, which, after a few weeks of fermentation, would become transformed into something altogether more moody and mysterious than its parent. In exchange for access to the press, local farmers would lend machinery and manpower to World's End Farm when needed, and in this way my parents, who were perennially short of money, managed to limp along without having to sink everything they had into expensive farm equipment.

The barn also housed, with room to spare, a full winter's supply of hay and straw for the hundred head of Hereford cattle which belonged to the farm, and the mountain of bales, reaching almost to the roof, made a wonderful hideout not only for an agile, seclusion-seeking child, but also for the odd heavily pregnant cat, determined, as mother cats universally are, to bring her litter into the world in absolute secrecy. Inevitably, though, the word got out that a new litter of kittens had arrived (I hate to think how often I was the one who betrayed the proud mother and her blind and helpless babies) and despite their resourceful mother's desperate efforts to move them, one at a time, to safety, Dad would always find them. Waiting for her to get hungry and come to the kitchen door to ask for food, Dad would feed her, and then follow her stealthily until she gave herself away by returning to her brood. The next day the litter would be gone and the distraught mother would be left pacing up and down, calling heartrendingly to her babies and straining her ears for the sound of their muffled reply. No one would ever tell me with any directness what had become of them. "They've gone to a new home" was all I could ever squeeze out of Mama, but far from reassuring me, this explanation, so obviously vague and dismissive, only served to make me more anxious. Where would they live? Who would feed them? Could I visit them? How would they survive without their mother's milk?

I found the answer to these questions one evening in early summer as I sat high up in the branches of an old apple tree in the orchard behind the barn. A door at the back of the barn opened, and Dad emerged, carrying an old burlap grain sack. Unaware of my presence, he walked directly toward my tree and as he approached I could see that whatever was in the sack was alive, for I could see it moving; and as Dad approached the cattle trough at the base of my tree I could clearly hear the plaintive mewing of kittens. There was a long galvanized steel water trough in the shade beneath the tree, and Dad plunged the sack deep into it, holding it under the water. After a minute or two he lifted the sack out, opened it and glanced inside. He swore under his breath and then quickly thrust the sack back into the water. Taking no chances this time, he kept it immersed for several minutes before finally lifting it out. Then he walked over to the dunghill at the side of the cattle shed, kicked away some dung to make a hole, emptied out the contents of the sack and covered the hole over. I found the little bodies there, wet and lifeless, all smeared with manure from their makeshift grave.

Parents could lie. To protect their children, perhaps; quite possibly also to protect themselves; but the important thing was, parents could lie.

Dad was a rationalist through and through. He loathed religion: to him it was not only the opium of the people, it was hemlock, cyanide for the intellect. He had nothing but contempt, either, for anything that smacked of mysticism, from old wives' tales and superstitions to my childish fascination with ghosts and my consequent fear of the dark, from the brooding romanticism of certain nineteenth-century art and literature to the menacing gargoyles and prickly complexity of Gothic architecture. He believed that human reason was an irresistible force; that science would unlock every secret, cure every ill, and that human beings, by virtue of their rationality, were superior to all other forms of life. These were not simply elements of his general philosophy, they were credenda, and he clung to them fiercely and proclaimed them with a passion which was anything but rational.

In many ways it is not at all surprising that Dad gravitated first toward architecture and then toward farming, for both professions abound with opportunities to conscript and subdue nature, an activity in which the rationalist soul (such as it is) finds enormous solace.

Some of his earliest and most celebrated architectural works were zoo buildings, housing for captive animals, and although he later concentrated exclusively on large urban housing schemes for human occupation, those early zoo works remained unquestionably his personal favorites, for in them he was able to bring together many of the principles he held most dear. His animal houses were designed unapologetically as theaters, circuses; they made no attempt to simulate the natural habitat of their intended occupants. Instead, by juxtaposing the cool, mathematical precision of pure geometric shapes — cylinders, spirals, ellipses, cast in thin sections of white reinforced concrete — with the lumbering gait and awkward, unrefined behavior of the captive tenants, he made clowns and performers of them in spite of themselves. The animals became living monuments to rationalism, imprisoned not so much by bars or cages, but by their intellectual inferiority to humankind, whose hand had wrought the seamless, soaring concrete canopies that sheltered them.

Not that Dad was unsympathetic toward animals; far from it. He enjoyed their antics enormously, and was quite capable of showing them real tenderness, just as he was, indeed, with his children. But, as with his children, that tenderness was capricious and evanescent, dispensed out of some vague sense of noblesse oblige, and subject to abrupt and complete withdrawal. This capacity to give and withhold affection at will made him an impossible and at times profoundly cruel father, of course, but it was undoubtedly a great asset when it came to farming; for to the farmer, animals are first and foremost crops, commodities; there can be no room for squeamishness or sentimentality.

Dad approached the business of agriculture with the zeal and detachment of a scientist. Factory farming had not then been invented, but he discovered it for himself, turning his architectural skills to the task of designing slat-floored prisons in which to raise veal calves, and restrictive pens in which pigs and cows could be immobilized and forcibly, repeatedly mated to ensure the best yield of offspring with the least fallow time.

He designed a ghastly contraption, too, called a cattle crush — and it meant what it said. It consisted of a tall-sided, narrow, blind alley, with walls built of railroad ties embedded vertically in a concrete base. It was just wide enough to accommodate a cow, and once the unfortunate animal had been led into it, a steel gate slammed shut hard on its haunches, cramming the cow into a vise-hold from which it was powerless to escape. Thus paralyzed, the animal had no choice but to submit to whatever indignity its intellectual superiors had in store for it, from having its horns burned down to stumps with a red-hot polling iron to having its testicles removed — without anesthesia, of course, since the appreciation of pain was an exclusively human proclivity.

These things filled me with dread and horror. To me, there was never any doubt that the animals suffered, Mama's breezy denials notwithstanding. "It's just that they don't like being confined," she said; "but it's only for a moment and then they forget all about it. Besides, they don't feel pain like we do; they're only animals, after all." I knew then that I was entirely alone in my misgivings, and, moreover, that it would pay me to keep quiet about them in future, for if Dad were to get wind of my tenderheartedness he would surely pillory me again, the way he had when I caught him beating one of the cats for some misdemeanor or other, and protested vigorously to him. "Save your sympathy for the human race!" he had snapped, and then proceeded to subject me to scathing criticism in front of the rest of the family for indulging in romanticism and sentimentality, the archenemies of reason, truth and scientific progress. (Although exactly how reason, truth and scientific progress were being well served by his beating the living daylights out of a small tabby cat I was neither brave enough nor stupid enough to ask.) Fervent anti-individualist that he was, Dad expected his children to mirror his beliefs, and to do so enthusiastically. Any dissent or deviation was viewed not just as a sign of intellectual degeneracy but also as a deliberate act of disloyalty toward him. If he held a certain point of view, then so must we, and if he didn't like something it was axiomatic that we shouldn't, either.

And so I kept my own counsel and took the coward's

way out, suppressing my feelings of anger and revulsion and trying wherever I could to avoid witnessing any of the savage rituals of farming life. This wasn't always possible, though; the Lubetkin children were the only permanent farmhands at World's End Farm, and often, when the veterinarian visited, we were called upon to corner his patients and help hold them down while he did his awful work. Fear of incurring Dad's wrath and my siblings' derision thus proved stronger than my moral qualms, and I did my part, hating myself all the while for my faintheartedness and complicity.

There was no escaping, either, from the annual cattle roundup. Calling in all their cider-press favors, Dad and Mama would assemble a gang of ten or fifteen farmhands on loan from neighboring farms, but even this many men wasn't enough, and inevitably Sasha, Steve and I would be required to participate also. The cattle had to be rounded up from all the outlying fields and brought together in the old orchard behind the barn. In order to do this successfully, all possible escape routes had to be sealed off — and that was why so many able-bodied helpers, large and small, were needed. For once the cattle had been let loose from their fields and driven down into the valley toward the barn, they began stampeding, and there was a risk that the herd would simply turn and head off en masse in the opposite direction. The brawny farmhands, armed with stout sticks (which they had alarmingly few compunctions about using) were there to police the assembly and make sure that not a single cow or calf escaped — and none ever did.

Once the herd had been crowded into the orchard and

the gate had been shut behind them, the process of selection began. One by one, the cows would be brought from the orchard into the closed-off farmyard, and there Mama and Dad — and usually Alf Chapel as well, who had a skilled eye in such matters — would examine them, assessing their worth. How many more productive years has this one got left? How many more calves will she be able to bear? That one miscarried last year; she's got to go — too much of a liability. That one could do with fattening up; keep her back a year, maybe she'll calve next spring. That one's a good weight: she can go. The number of cows in the orchard dwindled as the number in the farmyard rose, and all the while there was a tension in the air, a suffocating sense of disquiet, a fretting and a mounting chorus of mooing as mothers were separated from their calves and the farmyard became more and more thronged.

At some point there would be a head count, and it would be determined that a sufficient number of the herd had been singled out. Then the tall-sided cattle truck, which had been parked across the driveway as an additional barricade, was maneuvered into the entry of the farmyard. The back of the truck was flung open, a ramp was let down, and the loading began. This invariably sparked panic, the cows seeming to sense that they were hopelessly trapped, but trying, nevertheless, to turn and run in a desperate bid to avoid being swallowed up by the yawning darkness ahead of them. The men encircled the hapless animals, beating and clubbing them, forcing them forward up the ramp. Soon the truck would be crammed to capacity, and the last cow, panting with fear, pushed aboard by the closing of the rear gates. The ramp would be lifted and locked in place, and the truck would pull away.

Did I believe Mama when she told me that those cows were just going to market, where they would be bought by another farmer? The first time, maybe. But I had seen the once-placid brown eyes, now dilated with terror, staring accusingly out at me through the air vents in the side of the truck, and I had lain awake at night after the cows had gone, listening to the mournful lowing of the lucky ones in the orchard behind the barn, the ones who, because they were still useful, had been allowed to stay — until the next time. I knew what the cows knew: that something unspeakable was about to happen to them, and no amount of circumlocution on Mama's part could bring me comfort. Eventually she stopped even trying. "Come on, darling, don't dwell on it," she said, sheepishly patting my back. "In the midst of life we are in death. They're only animals, after all."

$\mathcal{C}$ h a p t e r

6

๑๐ Of the two other houses at Upper Killington, one belonged to Alf Chapel, but was occupied by two weather-beaten and imponderably old men — brothers, by name of Arthur and George Stinchcomb — who had worked all their lives for Alf's father, and to whom Alf had let the house in perpetuity, on a handshake and for a peppercorn rent, by way of thanks. It was almost impossible to tell them apart, except that Arthur was stone deaf. They were devoted to each other for the most part, but every now and then they would quarrel (cider was invariably to blame) and then George's angry voice could be heard from one end of the valley to the other, while Arthur just sat there impassively, his brother's bellowed imprecations falling all around him as harmlessly and silently as snowflakes.

The other house, larger and altogether grander than either World's End or the home of the Stinchcomb brothers, stood empty for several years during my early childhood. Sasha said it was haunted, and even though Dad heaped scorn and ridicule on her for indulging in mysticism and superstitious fantasies, I had no doubt at all that she knew what she was talking about, especially since I myself had had an encounter there which put me in mortal fear of the place. I had wandered into its walled front garden, attracted by the perfect crimson peonies which still flowered bravely amid the chaotic crush of towering grass and loud, rampaging weeds. Wading through the undergrowth, I had disturbed a large snake, which reared up and struck at me, missing me by a hairbreadth. Terror-stricken, I dropped my fragrant booty and ran home.

The house had belonged to a farmer whose family had been hit by tragedy. His wife had died, suddenly and very young; his two sons had been killed in the war, and his only daughter had fallen in love with an American airman, got married (against her father's wishes) and gone to live in the United States. He never saw her again. Unable to face a lonely old age in the house which had once held all his hopes, he had moved away, abandoning the house but never letting go of it, until he finally died, and his executors put the house up for sale.

Ghosts notwithstanding, the house was bought by a wealthy couple, Charles and Elspeth Hamilton-Leigh, who belonged to that segment of upper-class English society into which Mama, too, had been born, and from which she had so early and so resolutely disassociated herself. Their passion was horses and hunting, and Upper Killington, which was situated in the heart of some of the most perfect foxhunting country in England, well within striking distance of the Beaufort Hunt's weekly meets, couldn't have suited them better. They had not bargained, however, on my parents, who hated everything they stood for; and while Mama, diplomat that she was, would surely rather have kept her contempt a family joke, safely confined within the four walls of World's End, Dad had no such scruples: peaceful coexistence meant nothing to him. He picked a fight with the Hamilton-Leighs at the first opportunity, and although the substance of the quarrel was never revealed to me in any detail, the end result was a mandatory and absolute family boycott. I was forbidden to have anything whatever to do with our new neighbors, which would have been no deprivation at all to me but for the fact that they had twin daughters my own age, with whom I, hungry for companionship and eager, besides, to learn to ride, had quickly struck up a promising friendship. Their house, full of the smell of saddle soap and old leather, and decorated at every turn with prints of regimental uniforms and Victorian hunting scenes, was thereafter out of bounds for me, and I never set foot in it again. The snake had clearly been an omen.

I suspected at the time (although I would never have had the audacity to suggest such a thing openly) that Dad had deliberately sabotaged relations with the Hamilton-Leighs in order to prevent what he saw as undesirable influences coming to bear on his family, and on me in particular, since it was I who had courted their company. Even before the quarrel, Dad had imposed severe restrictions on the amount of time I was permitted to spend with them. I was allowed one hour, no more than twice per week, and Dad timed that hour to the minute, setting his watch as I ran off down the hill to their house, and checking it conspicuously when I returned. Inevitably there were occasions on which I lost track of time; I was eight years old, after all, and had not yet fully surrendered myself to being ruled by the clock. Realizing with a sudden lurch of anxiety that I had overspent my statutory play allowance, I would drop everything at once and bolt for home, bending double as I passed under the kitchen window so as to avoid being seen by Dad, creeping in the back door and tiptoeing silently upstairs to my bedroom, hoping against hope that he hadn't noticed my absence. But of course he had, and my clumsy attempt to avoid detection only served to make the retribution fiercer.

It did not pay to argue with Dad. He had an explosive temper, and nothing triggered it more inexorably than being defied by one of his children. It made no difference if he was clearly in the wrong, or if the issue was entirely trivial: he simply could not tolerate dissent. You knew it was too late the second you opened your mouth. "IDIOT!" he would roar at you, in his thick Russian accent, whipping his glasses off and glaring at you with bulging eyes, contempt and fury combining to harden his features into something resembling a samurai war mask. There was no stopping him then: although he lost his composure with frightening ease, it often took him days to regain it, and during that time you were a pariah. He would neither speak to you nor look at you, and if you should happen to touch him he would flinch, pulling sharply, disgustedly away from you as though you were leprous.

He punished all transgressions, no matter how minor, by turning cold in this way, and the restoration of peace required of the offender a painfully long drawn-out process of self-abasement and ever more abject apologizing, until finally Dad would signal a thaw by delivering a solemn monologue about the fragility of love — parental love included — and the dangers of putting it to the test. "Love is like a wall," he would say, drawing a splendidly bathetic architectural analogy, "and each time there is a quarrel a new crack appears, a chunk of mortar crumbles. In time, the wall becomes so weak that it simply collapses, and once it has fallen it can never be rebuilt the way it used to be." Naturally he saw himself as the one whose love was being tested to the limit; it never occurred to him, I am sure, that his children might identify with the wall in his analogy, casting him as the cracker of stones and the crumbler of mortar. He was nothing if not vain.

Nor was he willing to let bygones be bygones once a quarrel had finally come to an end. He often nursed grievances for long periods, returning to them again and again as if to whet the pain which might otherwise long since have dulled and died away. Hidden behind the books on the top shelf in his study he kept a series of notebooks — dubbed by us the Book of Grievances — in which he chronicled our wrongdoings, omissions and shortcomings. Writing sometimes in Russian, sometimes in English and sometimes in a mixture of the two, he recorded incidents of such banality that it is difficult to imagine how they could have precipitated the seismic and seemingly unquenchable anger that they did.

Three apples on kitchen table at breakfast; only two left at lunchtime. I questioned Steven, who repeatedly denied taking apple, but was obviously lying because he blushed.

Louise's bed unmade despite two reminders.

Sasha stole piece of fudge from kitchen.

He viewed these misdemeanors, inconsequential as they truly were, not as random childish peccadillos but as sinister portents, symptoms of an underlying malaise; and he saw himself as the benign, concerned physician, carefully watching his afflicted patients and collecting clinical evidence, the better to assess their pathology and devise effective treatments.

Often the precise nature of the original transgression would become overshadowed by its supposed significance as a marker for something deeper and more ominous, and one would find oneself being asked to apologize not for the taking of an apple without permission but for the essential mediocrity of one's character. It was not uncommon, either, to be accused of something one had not done, and yet to incur Dad's wrath nonetheless, simply on account of the spiritedness of one's denial — vehemence being a quality which the good doctor, although himself a master of the art, could not abide in others. We were children of Stalinism, and we very early learned that one didn't necessarily need to have done anything; attitudes were even more important than actions, since attitudes were truer windows on one's ideological and intellectual development, and sensitive barometers of its orthodoxy.

It was in these situations above all that we would turn to

Mama for support, begging her to intercede on our behalf. And this, with great selflessness and not a little raw courage, she would do, pleading with Dad to be gentler to his children, and not to draw such sweeping conclusions about their worth on the basis of such tenuous evidence. Inevitably, this would cause him to turn the full force of his wrath on her like a water cannon, for, as he saw it, she was willfully opposing him — an act that showed her to be as shallow and disloyal as the children themselves, and deserving of no lesser punishment. Their voices would be heard coming from the kitchen, Mama's measured appeals crowded out and shouted down by Dad's relentless harangue. And whichever one of us it was who had unleashed Dad's fury would listen at the kitchen door, or creep across the uneven floor of my bedroom, which was directly above the kitchen, praying for the creaky floorboards to stay silent, and would make use of the numerous cracks between the boards to observe the proceedings taking place below.

To watch oneself being tried by kangaroo court in this way was a terrible experience: the sense of utter powerlessness was overwhelming. But worse by far was to witness Dad's deliberate cruelty to Mama, the way he berated her and called her an idiot, the way he reduced her to tears and made her sob so heartrendingly, all to punish her for taking her child's part instead of his. That was truly unbearable. Despite the murderous hatred we felt for him at these times, all that really mattered to us was to alleviate Mama's suffering, and if that meant apologizing profusely — even for something we hadn't done — and subjecting ourselves to remorseless self-criticism, so be it: for her sake we would acknowledge the trumped-up charges, sign the confession, admit to being enemies of the people.

But Dad was an autocrat in the true Russian tradition: an extraordinary union of heartlessness and humanity; Cossack cruelty coexisting with grand sentimentality; the knout in one hand, the balalaika in the other; and the man who could arouse both abject fear and incandescent resentment in his children could also inspire them with an insatiable hunger for his affection. The father who denigrated his children without mercy and harbored festering grievances against them was also the father who could disarm them with a sudden kindness, embrace them with his ready laughter, beguile them by blowing smoke rings and wiggling his ears, and play the piano for them like Paderewski, throwing open the windows of the old farmhouse and filling the entire valley with the cascading, kaleidoscopic music of Chopin.

Mama was as bewitched by him as we were, and it was she who fed and fueled the natural longing we had to be loved by him, and who shielded the flame and kept it alive when his volatile temper and blistering anger threatened to extinguish it entirely. She it was, too, who insisted against all the evidence that he did indeed love us, and that if only we knew him better — *really* knew him, as she did — then we would understand what made him the monster he could sometimes be, and would forgive him for it. "One day," she said, "he'll explain everything to you. Then you'll understand."

☙

One thing is certain: the people who thought they knew Dad didn't know him at all, and that was as true for his children as it was for the few friends he and Mama still kept. Only Mama really knew him, really understood him, but her understanding of him owed more to faith than to insight: she simply accepted him unquestioningly, recognizing his faults but giving them no weight. And although she knew him inside out she kept that knowledge doggedly to herself, meeting my every plea for an explanation with a curious reticence, and quietly insisting that Dad must be the one to tell his story, and no one else. This meant, of course, that the story never got told, and that was exactly the way Dad wanted it, for he was clearly not inclined to explain himself to anyone, least of all to his children. Indeed, on the few occasions when I plucked up courage and made timid overtures in that direction, he jumped at the chance to tell me that he considered me too stupid to understand anything more challenging than Mickey Mouse — a taunt which Mama, in her usual placatory way, dismissed as merely Dad's clumsy attempt at humor, but which stung and bruised me nonetheless, causing me to shy away from asking any question which might invite a similar rebuff.

Being the youngest, I had had ample opportunity to watch my brother and sister battling their way through childhood ahead of me, and I harbored few illusions as to what lay in store for me. I was therefore a great deal more interested in avoiding conflict with Dad than I was in plumbing his psychology. And even if there was, as Mama had so often told me, some mitigating explanation for his fulminant temper and tyrannical behavior, it was largely academic as far as I was concerned. After all, this was by no means the only mystery surrounding Dad: almost nothing about him was straightforward or simple. Even his personal history was shrouded in obscurity. Whereas Mama was forever recounting stories of her childhood, her schooling, her aunts and uncles, cousins and grandparents, Dad never spoke about his family at all, and would not be drawn on the subject. And while Mama kept a photograph album full of pictures of her family, from the straitlaced, scowling Victorian worthies of her grandparents' generation all the way through her own childhood and right up to the time she met Dad, there was no corresponding album for Dad's side. Indeed, I never saw a single photograph of Dad's family, nor any of him as a child. It was almost as though his life had begun only upon his arrival in England in 1930. Before that there was no trace, no record and to all intents and purposes, no memory.

The little I knew about Dad's past I gleaned from Mama, who, with the evasiveness and palpable discomfort which characterized our conversations about Dad (she clearly felt that she was somehow being disloyal to him), told me only that he had been born in 1901 in czarist Russia, that he had been the child of a wealthy family with homes in St. Petersburg and Moscow, and that the family had been wiped out by the Bolsheviks in the Russian Revolution of 1917. Dad was the only survivor.

I forget how old I was when Mama first imparted this information to me — six, maybe, or seven — but I do remember that it troubled me enormously, evoking a deep compassion for Dad which ran entirely counter to the cringing submissiveness he typically inspired, and serving to worsen the miserable ambivalence I felt toward him. As I grew older, of course, and began to fight more and more fiercely with him, that compassion withered, and in its place there arose a great bitterness toward him for remaining a communist in spite of the fact that his family had been butchered on the altar of Marxism, and a silent, angry cynicism toward the ideology he so obstinately espoused.

Just about the only aspect of Dad's past about which there was no doubt, and of which he made no secret, was that Berthold Lubetkin was not his real name. This he freely admitted, although, even so, neither he nor Mama would ever reveal what his real name was. He had acquired the name, he told me, in order that he could enter the University of Warsaw to study architecture. It was at a time shortly after the Russian Revolution, when a tide of nationalistic fervor was sweeping through Poland, a country which lay open and vulnerable on the western doorstep of the emerging Soviet Union. In an attempt to shore up its independence and guard against being engulfed by the civil war that was still raging unabated inside Russia, the Polish authorities decreed that Soviet citizens would not be allowed to reside in Poland, nor attend Polish universities; these privileges would be reserved exclusively for Poles. Since Dad was then still a Soviet citizen, it became imperative for him to acquire Polish nationality at once, and he did so by clandestinely purchasing the name and forged identity papers of a long-dead Polish citizen, one Berthold

Lubetkin, native of Warsaw. Newly minted citizenship in hand, he entered and duly graduated from the University of Warsaw, leaving his real name behind forever.

While I understood almost instinctively that the secrecy surrounding Dad's real name sprang from his need to put the painful memory of the fate of his family firmly behind him, I was nevertheless fascinated by the whole idea of his assumed identity. There was something intriguing and glamorous about it, and I used to daydream endlessly about what our real family name might be, who we really were, and why it had to be kept such a profound secret. In my mind's eye, depending on how well or badly Dad and I happened to be getting along, I would imagine him as the last of the Romanovs, hiding his royal ancestry behind a commoner's name; or he would be a heartless criminal, like Raskolnikov in Dostoyevsky's *Crime and Punishment*, hoping to escape the consequences of his own villainous past.

And so Dad remained a complete enigma to me, a man entirely made up of contradictions and inconsistencies, a man who had no qualms about preaching one thing with passionate conviction whilst practicing quite the opposite; a man who systematically isolated himself behind a wall of secrecy, emerging only to punish, criticize or pass judgment on his children. The wonder of it is not that I lived in fear of him, but that I so desperately wanted him to love me, and would go to the most extraordinary lengths to please him. But his praise was always fleeting. He dispensed affection as though it were a cash payment to an odd-jobber: no promises, no long-term commitment; you did it right this time, but that doesn't mean I consider you reliable.

Knowing that I could only earn his love on piecework, I constantly sought ways to prove myself useful to him. Quietly and unbidden I would empty his ashtray, polish his shoes, bring him cups of coffee, being called a creep by my brother and sister, and incurring their jealousy for the small gratuity of affection Dad would occasionally pay me for my attentiveness. I was fiercely proud of the nickname he gave me — *kurrinny eyes* ("chicken eyes" in Russian) — for my sharp-sightedness and my useful ability to find even tiny objects which had been misplaced. To me it seemed such a milestone: I had earned myself a permanent place in his life at last.

How ironic it is that my most treasured gift from him is one he never intended that I should have, and which I therefore never dared mention to him, still less thank him for. I was only eight or nine at the time, but the memory of that strange incident has stayed with me ever since, luminous and powerful. Late one night I stirred from a deep sleep to find Dad sitting beside my bed, gently stroking my hair. He thought I was still fast asleep, of course, but I wasn't. There was a full moon that night, and in its light I could clearly see the tears which filled his eyes and trickled down his cheeks. "You look so much like my mother," he whispered. Then he kissed my forehead and quietly slipped out of the room.

After he'd gone I lay awake for a long time listening to the slow, sad sound of a Chopin nocturne coming softly from the piano downstairs.

Chapter
7

How much simpler it would all have been if only I could have hated Dad, hated him consistently and without wavering, instead of veering miserably from one extreme to the other, never quite being able to let go of love even in the thick of loathing! But that was precisely the measure of his power, for he could both tyrannize and enchant with supreme virtuosity, and his charm — rare, unexpected and insubstantial as a rainbow — was all the more magical for being so fleeting.

Of course, people outside the family never knew of his cruel and authoritarian side. Janus that he was, he hid it from them, saving it exclusively for his nearest and dearest, and the Berthold Lubetkin other people knew was a delightful, entertaining man who enthralled them with his nimble mind, original outlook and witty conversation. Even my teachers, although undoubtedly they found the intrusion of Dad's communist ideology into my schoolwork irritating and even mildly alarming, were captivated by him on the few occasions their paths crossed, at PTO meetings and suchlike. They never suspected, I am sure, what sort of father he really was, nor what torments he inflicted on his children behind closed doors in that lonely old farmhouse at Upper Killington.

Certainly I never breathed a word to them about him. I wouldn't have dared, since to have done so would have been a clear breach of the strict code of loyalty which Dad had inculcated in us, and which governed all our dealings with the world outside Upper Killington. The rules were few and simple: under no circumstances were any of us to discuss family matters (and the definition of what constituted family matters was all-encompassing) with outsiders. In a hideous emulation of Stalinist revolutionary vigilance, Dad set us to watch over one another and to denounce one another for any perceived infringements, for which he would then devise a suitable punishment. This varied in minor detail, but always involved a period, sometimes lasting several days, of absolute ostracism, during which the offender was zealously excluded from every aspect of family life. Spoken to by no one, arbitrarily deprived of meals, forced to sit in silence while other members of the family took turns to express their disgust for the transgressor's disloyalty — who would be brave (or foolhardy) enough to risk the consequences of breaking the Lubetkin family *omertà* for the sake of a little sympathy from a schoolteacher?

Besides, would sympathy even have been forthcoming? Probably not; after all, who would have believed that the congenial and charismatic Berthold Lubetkin the outside world knew was actually someone else entirely, someone who imposed intolerable emotional burdens on his children and ruled their lives with a rod of iron? And who could have blamed the world for its incredulity? Heaven knows I myself hardly knew from day to day what I felt about him, so hopelessly ambivalent was I. For although there were countless occasions when I seethed with rage and resentment, and longed to proclaim Dad's tyrannies and injustices from the rooftops, there were also a good many others when I basked in his affection like a lazy cat in a summer garden, and at those times, brief though they were, all wrongs seemed righted and all misgivings quelled.

Nevertheless, living in a perpetual state of vertiginous uncertainty and suppressed anger took its toll on me, and, not for the last time in my life, my body decided to speak up indignantly on behalf of my muzzled and beleaguered mind. I began having crippling stomachaches for which no immediate physical cause could be found, and which therefore quickly earned me Dad's unbridled displeasure on account of what he saw as a cut-and-dried case of malingering. He accused me of histrionics and dubbed me Sarah Bernhardt, after the crown princess of stage and silent movie melodrama. What's more, he encouraged Sasha and Steve to pick up the nickname and taunt me with it, which, eager for any means, however ignoble, to earn Dad's approval, they cheerfully did.

Once, in the grip of a particularly bad attack, I flopped to the ground in a cold faint and had to be fetched home from school in the middle of the day, something that Dad regarded as an enormous imposition at the best of times, although quite why he felt that way I have never been able to fathom. He had nothing much else to do: no office to go to, no pressing work which must take priority. Indeed, he spent most days sitting at the kitchen table reading, listening to the radio and talking to Mama, or closeted in his den, surrounded by books. Perhaps he felt ill at ease in the role of gentleman farmer — a profession which would surely have earned him a bullet in the head back in his motherland — and felt the need to pretend to be considerably busier than he truly was. Whatever the reason, he fiercely resented being at his children's beck and call, and interpreted my stomachaches as nothing more or less than a crude and deliberate attempt on my part to dictate to him. He drove me home from school that day at breakneck speed, the thunderous, pulsating silence between us broken only by the crashing of the gears. He was an awful driver anyway, but in a towering rage he lost any semblance of patience and coordination, and seemed to abandon the clutch entirely.

Mind you, he was not much more sympathetic when any of us fell prey to illnesses with undeniable physical symptoms and cast-iron microbial credentials. He viewed anything that deflected Mama's attention from its faithful and exclusive focus on him as a direct challenge to his supremacy, and reacted accordingly. Sickness therefore meant banishment, pure and simple: no food (sick people don't eat); no visitors (if you want company you can't possibly be feeling ill); and absolutely no calling out for Mama, not even for the last rites. I remember coming down with an impressive case of chicken pox and dealing with it more or less on my own, Dad's only concession to my plight being to permit Mama to bring me a cup of bouillon and a piece of dry toast each lunchtime, and to order my hands encased in thick woolen socks so as to thwart the scratching which had become my sole diversion during those long, wretched days.

Poor Sasha, on whom Andrew's proclivity for tonsillitis seemed, by some eerie quirk of fate, to have been visited, frequently found herself an exile because of it. I remember hearing her crying once, alone in her darkened leprosarium, and creeping in, against all the rules, to visit and comfort her. It was Mama she wanted, of course, but that was out of the question, and she knew better than to call out for her. How terrible it must have been for Mama, too, who never got over her grief at the loss of Andrew, and who, I know, carried a crushing burden of guilt for having invited his death by consigning him, tiny and helpless, to the care of an incompetent surgeon. But Dad's directives were not open to discussion, and his opinion was that one should err on the side of punishing, rather than pampering, the sick, on grounds that pandering to their wants and needs would only make the sickbed more attractive. Visits from Mama for anything other than essential purposes, or for any longer than a minute or two, smacked to him of brazen indulgence, and he would not permit it. Vigilant and omnipresent, he would come to the foot of the stairs, stand there listening for a moment, and then, in the exaggeratedly slow and menacing tone of someone scolding a disobedient dog, his voice rising inquisitorially on the last syllable, "Ma-*maaa?*" he would call. It was all that was needed.

The fact that Dad was so extraordinarily healthy himself surely cannot have helped to imbue him with a spirit of compassion for the sick. He almost never succumbed to illness. Even common colds seemed to bounce off him, and in all the years we lived at World's End I don't remember him ever taking to his bed for any reason. He claimed that he had never thrown up in his life, even as a child, and I think he may well have been telling the truth. Certainly that would go some way toward explaining why he had so little patience and sympathy for those of us whose constitutions were less robust than his own. Illness irritated him; he saw it as a form of moral flaccidity, even disloyalty — yes, disloyalty, for if he could resist disease, shrug it off and refuse to be laid low by it, then so could we, and if we failed to do so it could only be because of a basic lack of fidelity to his leadership and example.

Disloyalty haunted him, and since he was constantly on the lookout for it, he found it all around him, often in the most prosaic and unlikely places. It was a great mistake, for example, to let it be known that one disliked any food of which Dad happened to be fond, for he would interpret such an admission as clear evidence that one was bent on rejecting his values, lock, stock and barrel. He would react by declaring that one was unfit to be his child or even to bear his name. "You are a non-'betkin," he would pronounce, having first, of course, praised and congratulated the others lavishly for being such good, loyal " 'betkins," a crude but effective technique which was calculated to magnify the sense of loneliness and exclusion suffered by the errant, unworthy child.

Of all the foods I could have found unpalatable, therefore, it was particularly unfortunate for me that I had a passionate and abiding dislike of beets, for beets are a staple of Russian cooking, and Dad loved them. Mama, knowing how much Dad loved them, went out of her way to grow them in abundance in the kitchen garden; there was never any shortage of them, and they appeared on the table with depressing frequency. I tried quietly begging Mama to take pity on me and serve me smaller portions, but my machinations backfired horribly: Dad caught her doing as I had asked and realized at once that he had uncovered a conspiracy. The rebuke I incurred was predictably bitter and painful, to be sure, but the real target of Dad's fury was Mama, who had connived with me in my disloyalty, and for her he reserved a special savagery, heaping accusation upon recrimination, scorn upon contempt, as though she had committed the foulest and most egregious act of treachery imaginable.

It cost Mama dearly to defend herself — or us — against this sort of onslaught, and, indeed, she often seemed to me simply to go limp, to let the barrage rain down upon her unopposed, perhaps in the hope that if she said nothing and remained still, it would eventually exhaust itself. And in the end, of course, it always did, though not without leaving its mark upon all of us. Sometimes, though, she was drawn into the fray in spite of herself, and when this happened she would do her damnedest to contain the situation by lowering her voice to an obtundent and passionless near-whisper. This had the magical effect of pulling Dad's voice down by several decibels, albeit temporarily. Mama was a mine of classical and biblical quotations, and "A soft answer turneth away wrath" was a special favorite of hers, being one whose veracity she had had ample opportunity to put to the test in the stormy environment of the Lubetkin family.

What I didn't know until much, much later was that many times she did indeed fight back, and spiritedly, on her own behalf as well as ours; but, loyal to a fault, she studiously — and misguidedly — kept these arguments away from us by indulging in them only when we were safely out of the house or fast asleep. In this way she avoided criticizing Dad or challenging the wisdom or fairness of his actions in front of us, something which, although it undoubtedly served to shore up Dad's ego and maintain his authority, often felt, from a child's perspective, uncomfortably akin to abandonment.

The infamous beet conspiracy, of course, was carefully documented by Dad in the Book of Grievances, but it was not until long after I had grown up and left home that I had the chance to read the entry that followed it:

Mama said to me, inter alia:

"If the role of a parent is to be a devil who terrorizes and bullies everyone, then I am indeed not a mother in this sense. No woman would have done a fraction of what I have done for you during the past twenty years. Constantly for your sake I have abandoned what I thought to be right and accepted your judgment against

my better self. Constantly I have done violence to my own con-
science on your account. You are always imposing your will, forc-
ing people to do what you want or think right; always
reprimanding, telling off and bullying. Who do you think you
are? What gives you the right to treat people like this? You see
nothing but sinister and dirty motives everywhere you look."

I wonder if Dad was as shaken by her words then as I was
all those years later. I think he must have been, because
Mama's voice is so clearly audible in the transcript of what
she said. Dad seems to have resisted the temptation, which
must have been strong, to slant or embellish what she said,
or to put words into her mouth in order to bolster his own
case and project himself as the injured party — and that
says to me that on some level, however deep and deter-
minedly inaccessible, he knew she was right.

I was not the only one to run up against Dad's culinary
shibboleths. Beets may have been my nemesis; Steve's was
butter, and that was in all respects more unfortunate, for
even in a good summer the kitchen garden could not sus-
tain a daily diet of beets, whereas butter was something
which turned up at almost every meal. Now Dad, for all his
declared faith in the dictatorship of the proletariat, had a
very pronounced appetite for the good things in life. He
was also an unregenerate intellectual snob, and intellectual snobbery is nothing more than plain old class snobbery masquerading as aestheticism and wearing a learned
frown. The butter Dad wanted on his table, therefore, could
not be the common or garden salted stuff which was stan-
dard fare at that time; it had to be the beautiful ivory-white

unsalted French butter, imported from Normandy. Its taste, he said, was far superior; the English butter was so coarse and unrefined it was not fit to eat — although, for simple reasons of economy, he did permit Mama to use English butter (or axle grease, as he contemptuously referred to it) for cooking.

Steve, on the other hand, loathed French butter, and craved the axle grease. This brought him into almost daily conflict with Dad, who was of the opinion that it was boorish and thoroughly pedestrian to choose English butter over French — and, of course, a brazen example of disloyalty. When tarring Steve with the non-'betkin label ceased, through sheer repetition, to have the desired effect, Dad began calling him "the village idiot" instead, slumping his shoulders, half-closing his eyes and letting his tongue loll in a pitilessly graphic and accurate imitation of a retarded Hawkesworth man, well known to all, who passed his days harmlessly snoozing under haystacks and mumbling incoherently at passersby. May God forgive me for the times I gave in to my longing for Dad's approval and affection by laughing long and loud at his cruel gibes.

Dad used to taunt Steve, too, without mercy, about his nose. Despite the fact that Steve's nose and Dad's were identical in every respect, right down to a mole apiece in exactly the same place on their respective right nostrils, Dad used to comment at every opportunity about how ugly and prominent Steve's nose was, and how he was going to take Steve to Vienna and make him have plastic surgery on it to abate its intrusive presence and bring it down to a more acceptable shape and size.

What this must have done to poor Steve's sense of self-worth I can hardly bear to contemplate, especially since Dad encouraged the rest of us to laugh at his savage comments by injecting a sly note of levity into them. In Vienna, he promised, a twinkle in his eye, the surgery is carried out not by physicians but by slot machines in the street. You stand there, insert copious schillings, and hey presto! the machine does the rest. Having thus cleverly disarmed his remarks, he effectively placed the onus for taking them to heart squarely on Steve.

The trouble was, Dad could be uproariously funny, and although he most often used his talent in the service of some cruel aim, bludgeoning us, ridiculing us, dividing us one from another, he was also quite capable of using it to bind us all together as a family, weaving a tenacious cocoon around us from which, try as I might, I have never managed to escape.

He was not afraid, either, to laugh at himself. In fact, one of his most endearing qualities was his ability to puncture his own pomposity and poke fun at himself. Sometimes, right in the middle of one of his philippics, he would suddenly see the farcical side of something he had said, and would hold it up to ridicule with an honesty and humor so disarming that one instantly forgave him all the bitterness and scathing criticism that had gone before. I remember being mercilessly browbeaten by him over something absolutely trivial which, as usual, he had overlaid with tremendous significance, seeing it as a symptom of something far larger and more ominous. On and on he ranted, his voice climbing, his fist pounding the table — and then, without warning, he said, "I am right. I am in no doubt whatsoever that I am right. In fact, I am so profoundly persuaded of my own rectitude that I must almost certainly be wrong." With that he dissolved into a mischievous giggle which instantly dispelled all anger and resentment in me, leaving me as much a prisoner of my love for him as I had been, only moments earlier, of my hate.

He was wildly irreverent, too, and loved nothing better than defying rules and deflating self-important petty officials. *Pour épater les bourgeois* (to shock the narrow-minded) was one of the first phrases I ever learned in French, and it was Dad who taught it to me, and Dad who showed me how to do it. Our family trips abroad during school vacations abounded with opportunities for him to practice this hazardous sport, since crossing from one country to another always entails brushes with officials — police, passport control, customs — who demand documents and examine them with *gravitas* in the hope of detecting undotted *i*'s or uncrossed *t*'s. Germany, for some reason, seemed to bring out the worst in Dad. Once — I think it was in Munich; maybe Cologne — he got hopelessly lost and needed to pull over to look at the map. He had been there no more than two minutes before a stone-faced Teuton resplendent in the uniform of the Bundespolizei walked up to the car, and, after tapping on the driver's side window, silently handed Dad a parking ticket. Dutifully, solemnly, Dad took the ticket from him, and, with great aplomb, stuffed it into his mouth and slowly chewed it up before driving wordlessly away.

Dad loved to play with words, and although he had known no English at all before his arrival in England at the age of thirty, he quickly learned to speak it with an astonishing fluency, mastering not only the mechanics of the language but also its quirks and inconsistencies, its bewildering idioms and a prodigious chunk of its vast and colorful vocabulary as well. He found rhymes irresistible, and produced them out of thin air, just for the fun of it. There was a point on the route home from Hawkesworth to Upper Killington where the road ran along the side of a hill, and from there one could see clear down the Severn valley, the hills stretching rhythmically off into the distance, to where England stopped and Wales began. Dad called this vista "the Spine," and composed a couplet in its honor:

> *Why do your eyes shine?*
> *Because I see the Spine . . .*

To this he soon added, with cheerful disregard for both scansion and plausibility:

> *Right along the line,*
> *Discovered by Doctor Klein*
> *And his girlfriend, Gertrude Stein.*
> *They came from Heidelberg on Rhine*
> *In the year nineteen hundred and thirty-nine,*
> *Bringing their pet porcupine*
> *Which was part human, part divine,*

> *Part amphibious, part canine;*
> *They kept it tied with baler twine,*
> *And fed it cucumbers pickled in brine....*

It became a family ritual to recite the Spine saga every time we traveled that road, and whatever conversation happened to be in progress at that point was summarily suspended while we chanted Dad's ode in unison. We were usually pulling into the driveway at World's End before we had finished.

He was also a wonderful storyteller. He created the character of Igor Kolashinski, detective, explorer and adventurer, inveterate gambler and bon vivant (yet tireless champion of the underdog, nevertheless), and kept us spellbound with stories of his exploits. Part of the magic was in the telling, of course: the stories were pure fantasy, but Dad delivered them with a steadiness and assurance that left one in no doubt that these were well-documented events that he himself had witnessed. And they were so graphic:

Igor Kolashinski angrily stubbed out his cheroot on the frictionless green baize of the billiard table, turned on his heel, and, brushing the obsequious doorman unceremoniously aside, strode out of the Aqualung Casino in the red-light district of Addis Ababa....

I have never forgotten these florid opening lines, nor the sound of Dad's deep voice as he spoke them, his Russian accent adding a portentous echo to every word. And even now I cannot take a train journey without being reminded of how the infinitely resourceful Kolashinski succeeded in stopping a runaway train by hanging precariously from the engine and peeing with astonishing accuracy onto the overheated brakes to cool them down.

Dad was nearing fifty when I was born, and by then he bore little resemblance to the dark-haired, well-dressed and decidedly handsome figure in the photographs taken at the time he and Mama had first met. My early memories of him are of a paunchy man with a shiny bald head, brown eyes and a furrowed face, a cigarette always alight between his nicotine-stained fingers. He seemed tall to me then, but that was probably just because I was young and very much in awe of him. In fact he was quite short; Mama was a full five inches taller than him even in her bare feet. She was always a little self-conscious about this, not because she minded being tall so much as because she was worried that it might be disconcerting for Dad to be shorter than his wife.

Dad wore glasses, but they spent more time in his hand than on his nose. He used them as a conductor does a baton, tapping them briskly on the table in a peremptory demand for silence, flourishing them in broad, rhythmic strokes as the pace and intensity of a conversation quickened, and jabbing them at one with an accusatory fervor in order to elicit a reaction or drive home a point. Above all, his glasses were a sensitive indicator of his mood: if they were on his nose one had little to fear, but if he suddenly whipped them off it was a sure sign of an imminent explosion. He needed to be entirely unencumbered if he was to lose his temper properly, and it would have been as unnatural for him to have hurled invective with his glasses on as it would have been for him to have gone to bed without removing his shoes. It was a habit, however, that he came to have cause to regret.

There were few things which plunged Dad into a fouler or more volatile mood than hunger, and Mama, knowing this, moved heaven and earth to ensure that he had a good, hot lunch every day at twelve-thirty sharp. It was little short of a disaster, therefore, if the coal stove in the kitchen would not cooperate, for the stove was not only a comforting provider of warmth in the otherwise unheated house, it was also the sole source of heat for cooking. One bleak November day, through nobody's fault but Dad's own, the coal stove quietly went out. Dad's first job in the morning was to riddle out the ashes and pour in an avalanche of fresh anthracite, but on this particular day he had simply forgotten to do it, a fact which contributed immeasurably to his ill humor, since he had no one to blame but himself. That didn't stop him, though, from casting around to find ways in which the rest of us had contributed, however obliquely, to the lateness of his lunch, and Steve provided the perfect target.

It was Steve's job to chop kindling wood from time to time, but since the stove was kept going day and night and needed relighting so rarely, it was an easy thing for him to forget. As luck would have it, of course, now, just when dry kindling wood was urgently needed, none had been cut, and Steve frantically set about chopping some, hoping against hope to get enough cut quickly so that Dad would never find out that the supply had actually been allowed to run out. But Dad, furious at Steve's apparent dallying, strode out to the woodshed to see for himself what new depths of ineptitude his village idiot ten-year-old son had plumbed. He sized up the situation in a second, and, whipping his glasses off, began roaring at Steve. "IDIOT!" he bellowed, brandishing his glasses angrily; "Don't try now to conceal the fact of your laziness. Those who don't work, don't eat: you will have no food for the entire day!"

At that very moment, Steve raised the axe, and, with the full force of his sublimated rage, brought it down hard on the log he had set on the block to be split. Dad suddenly uttered a sharp cry and staggered backwards, slumping against the wall. His hands were clapped to his face, and almost at once blood began trickling through his fingers. For a second Steve just stood there, the axe dangling from his hand, all color abruptly gone from his cheeks. He was convinced that he had committed a murder, and so was I; I had witnessed the whole thing from the doorway and now stood transfixed by the sight of my crumpled, bleeding father. I had never seen him in a position of helplessness before, and while I was terrified by what had happened, and by the thought of him dying, there was a part of me which found some dark satisfaction in the revenge that Steve had brought upon him. I was only seven then, and I had never heard of Oedipus, and I don't think Steve had, either, but the implications of the scene I had just witnessed were certainly not lost on me.

As it turned out, Dad was neither dead nor dying. He

had, though, sustained a bad injury when a splinter of wood from the log Steve was chopping had flown up and punctured his left eye. He spent the next four weeks in the hospital undergoing operation after operation to save his eye, and being reminded with relentless frequency and excruciating tactlessness by the medical staff that if only he had been wearing his glasses instead of holding them in his hand, none of this would ever have happened.

Mama, of course, was distraught about the accident, and terrified that Dad would lose his eye, which, initially at least, looked quite probable. She also just plain missed him: they had never been apart for more than a day or two at a time, and without him her life seemed to lack any real purpose or direction. Our lives, by contrast, had never felt freer, and even now those four weeks stand out in my memory as unquestionably some of the happiest of my childhood. World's End was an entirely different place under Mama's stewardship. Gone was the whispering, the tiptoeing, the listening at doors, the sense of being constantly judged and found wanting. Sasha tuned the radio to pop music stations and comedy shows which were strictly forbidden to us when Dad was at home, and Mama made no attempt to stop her. The house was suddenly full of singing and laughter. Mama played cricket on the front lawn with us, cooked us our favorite meals and let us eat as much or as little as we wanted. Steve gorged himself on axle grease and I spurned the dreaded beets with impunity. We played card games and hide-and-seek, and at night Mama came up to tuck me in and stayed with me, sitting on my bed and telling me stories as though that had always been her habit, while I resisted sleep with all my might, scared to miss a minute of her precious company.

Not that I was indifferent to Dad's plight; far from it. The sight of him half blind, marooned in his pajamas in that echoing open ward, surrounded by strangers and with nothing to call his own except a pitcher of tepid water on the nightstand by his bed upset me enormously, and I determined to bring him something from home, something to anchor him and remind him that he was my dad. Mama told me that it had to be something small because he had no room to keep anything, and I found the ideal thing: a tiny white plastic bear, no more than an inch tall, which, I was convinced, had magical powers — although I never would have dreamed of confiding this fact to my fervently rationalistic and antisuperstitious father. The little bear was my most treasured possession, and parting with him was extremely hard, but it had to be, and I handed him over to Dad's safekeeping with a heavy heart and great solemnity. "His name is King Siphon, Dad," I explained. "King Siphon?" he replied, looking quizzically at me with his good eye. He took one of the clean handkerchiefs which Mama had brought him, and after carefully wrapping King Siphon up in it, put the little bundle in the breast pocket of his pajamas. "King Siphon," he said again, patting his pocket.

A month after his injury Dad left the hospital, his sight miraculously intact, although the injured eye had completely changed color and was now a pupil-less and inscrutable pigeon gray, like a monocle. No longer able to tolerate much light, he had to wear dark glasses more or less constantly, something rarely seen in England, where the sun, in keeping with the national character, is generally rather shy and retiring, and tends not to force itself on people.

The dark glasses were the final straw as far as my schoolmates were concerned. Already suspicious of him because of his strange name and foreign accent, they were now convinced beyond doubt that Dad was a Russian spy (it was, after all, at the time of the Cold War), and they jeered at me and taunted me mercilessly, calling me a traitor and assuring me that my entire family would be caught and put in jail, and that Mama and Dad would be executed, and serve them bloody well right. Children are uniquely gifted when it comes to savaging one another's sensibilities.

There was no TV at that time in our house, and since Dad could no longer read for more than a few minutes without stopping to rest his eyes, Mama began to read aloud to him during the long winter evenings. She had a wonderful reading voice, and it very quickly became a family tradition to gather around the kitchen table after supper and listen to her. Never one to waste any opportunity to work, Mama knitted feverishly as she read, the needles clicking away seemingly without any conscious involvement on her part. She never took her eyes off the page or hesitated in her reading even when she sensed that she had dropped a stitch and had to go back to pick it up again. The choices of reading material usually went way above my young head — Tolstoy, Thackeray, Dostoyevsky, Dickens — and often I got hopelessly entangled in the tortuous plots and found myself not listening at all, but drifting in my own private world under the hypnotic spell of Mama's diligently fidgeting hands.

Occasionally Dad would interrupt Mama's flow to comment on a passage or a description he found particularly pleasing. "Marvelous. Bloody marvelous," he would say. "Like wine!" And Mama would reread the passage so he could enjoy it again. Of course I never really understood what it was that Dad found so remarkable in those snippets; I wasn't old enough or experienced enough to know good writing from bad, or to revel in the acuteness of a writer's powers of observation, the way he did. But there was one occasion on which he asked Mama to repeat a passage and the note of seriousness — even sadness — in his voice so startled me that I lifted my eyes at once from Mama's knitting and listened carefully.

The book was *Great Expectations*, by Dickens, and the passage Dad wanted so much to savor again came at a point in the book where the hero, Pip, had become the recipient of a generous endowment from an unknown benefactor, and had left the humble rural home of the unpretentious blacksmith Joe Gargery in order to live a life befitting a gentleman in London. Joe Gargery pays Pip a visit at his elegant London house, and Pip, desperately trying to conceal his humble origins from his newfound aristocratic friends, and attempting to reinvent himself as a man of substance and social standing, cringes with embarrassment at Joe's soot-stained, hardworking hands, his muddy work boots and his uncultivated speech and manners. He does everything in his power to rush Joe out of the house before his superior friends arrive — and Joe sees this, understands it and sadly accepts it as his lot, conceding that Pip is now a gentleman, a member of a different class and a different world, and that their shared past, when Joe acted as the orphan Pip's father, no longer binds them.

"Listen to that! Listen to that!" Dad enjoined us; "Do you hear that? Do you see how he rejects his own father? See how ashamed he is of his own father, how he rejects his own background and upbringing? Remember that!"

And remember it I did, not least out of alarm that Dad, in addition to all his other powers, had clearly now also become a mind reader, and had divined my feelings of shame and embarrassment about his funny name, his Russian accent and his dark glasses. He must have found out about my terrible secret disloyalty to him. What other reason could there possibly be for him to have set such store by that passage from *Great Expectations*?

$\mathcal{C}$ h a p t e r

8

⌒⌒ If there was one way a child of Dad's could be assured of earning herself a spell, however brief, in the warm glow of her father's approbation, it was by demonstrating a willingness to work. Dad considered a zeal for work to be the hallmark of a good communist in the making — although he, it must be said, exhibited a distinct preference for the managerial side of things. World's End was really quite a small farm, neither busy enough nor profitable enough to justify any permanent hired help, but even so there was always plenty of work which needed to be done, and therefore plenty of opportunity to earn points and prove one's ideological mettle. It was tough work, too, especially for a child, but that was all to the good, since the measure of approval paid out by Dad tended to be in direct proportion to the onerousness of the work done. From a very tender age, therefore, I hurled myself at hard work with a quixotic vigor, tackling jobs way beyond my size and strength, and refusing to admit defeat even when it was

obvious that I couldn't possibly accomplish what I had set
out to do.

Staggering under the prickly heft of a hay bale, I would
squelch my way doggedly through mud and manure so deep
that it easily engulfed my Wellington boots and sucked
them off my feet, leaving me barefoot and vulnerable, bent
double under my enormous load amid the jostling, hungry
cattle. Or, gingerly carrying a gigantic scythe at least as
sharp and intimidating as that of the Grim Reaper himself,
I would head resolutely toward a towering thicket of briers
and stinging nettles, determined to level it. Inevitably, the
predatory undergrowth would close ranks around me, claw-
ing at me, tearing and stinging, resisting my feeble swipes
and rebounding triumphantly to inflict a bloody revenge on
me. Of course it didn't do to cry: bravery was highly prized
in our family, and I had taught myself as a very small child
to overcome the urge to cry by reciting a mantra of my own
composition: "ai-ee-inty-pinty; ai-ee-inty-pinty" until the
pain passed. It worked extremely well, on the whole, but,
alas, only for pain of a bodily nature; there was — and is —
no ai-ee-inty-pinty for the soul.

Although she clucked sympathetically over my cuts and
bruises, it was clear that Mama was quietly proud of my
frenetic striving, and she did little to discourage me. She
was a firm believer in the redemptive power of hard work,
and was herself the very model of diligence, self-sacrifice
and unceasing industry. "When the revolution comes," she
was fond of saying — only half jokingly — "they'll look at
your hands, and if you don't have blisters they'll stand you
up against a wall and shoot you." By way of illustration she

would hold out her own amazingly long-fingered hands, palms upward, upon which were visible an impressive assortment of scars and calluses, stigmata of years spent lovingly toiling in laundry, field and kitchen.

Lumpy hands were not Mama's only battle scars. In the course of heaving hundredweight sacks of grain around, climbing haystacks and digging trenches, she had developed a series of slipped disks and chronic back problems, the pain from which must have been truly agonizing, since she was eventually driven to seek orthopedic help — something she, being the most stouthearted and stoical person it is possible to imagine, would never have countenanced had she not been *in extremis*. On several occasions she was admitted to the hospital and spent several days there undergoing traction to ease the pain.

I clearly remember the utter desolation of World's End without her: the coldness, the silence, the cheerlessness. I would get to sleep at night only by pretending that she was downstairs in the kitchen, as usual, with Dad, and I would awaken each morning full of inconsolable anguish at the realization that she wasn't in the house after all. Sasha, who was then in her mid-teens, did her best to take Mama's place, cooking for Dad, Steve and me, and trying to make sure our basic needs were met. "Substitute Mama," Dad called her then, and that may well have been the most complimentary thing he ever said to her. Certainly she took the title very seriously, and maybe found her own comfort in it as she sat in Mama's chair at the kitchen table. But I couldn't forget the little rhyme which Mama used to recite to me in lighthearted reproof when she thought I was being a bit too demanding:

Be gentle to your mother and treat her with great care,
For you'll never know her value 'til you see her empty chair.

As far as I was concerned, there could be no substitute, and Mama's chair was sacrosanct.

Her return home from the hospital was always a joyous occasion for all of us, not least for Mama herself, who detested being separated from Dad, and who, like him, loved World's End with a passion. She came back from the hospital after one particularly long stay encased from shoulder to hip in a full plaster cast which chafed at her skin and forced her to move with the ossified, imperious gait of a Victorian governess. But even that didn't stop her from doing what she always did, first thing, in celebration of returning home after an absence: going upstairs to their bedroom and lying gratefully on the bed, listening to the skylarks and reveling in the fact of being back in that dear old house. Unable to let her out of my sight, I followed her upstairs and crept into the bedroom to be with her. It was summer, and for once it was really hot; the room was full of the smell of flowers wafting up from the garden beneath the open window, and Mama lay there, eyes closed, smiling to herself, dreamily dissecting the airborne bouquet into its many components. "Lavender, jasmine, alyssum . . . no, that's viburnum."

Her plaster cast didn't stop her working, either, and neither did the dire admonitions of her orthopedist. She was happy only when she was working. Any work would do; it didn't matter how menial. Work gave her a sense of dignity and self-worth, while idleness left her feeling wretched and superfluous.

Quite how Mama had come to embrace such a grim,

Stakhanovite vision of her own worth and purpose I can only guess. Certainly the communist faith to which she and Dad subscribed had a great deal to do with it, as, very possibly, did her childhood exposure to Christianity. For although she early and unequivocally rejected Christianity's spiritual message, its moral teachings remained very much a part of her, and in many ways she lived a more profoundly Christian life than do a great number of those who profess themselves to be devout believers. I remember her telling me that life was composed of a series of struggles against selfishness, and that one must never allow one's own wants or needs to come before those of others' — a dictum which she put sedulously into practice, especially where Dad was concerned. Indeed, so thoroughly did she efface herself, the better to anticipate and cater to his every need, that she seemed eventually to lose all awareness of her own needs, coming instead to live and define herself entirely through her service to husband and family. Under these circumstances work of any sort must have taken on an exaggerated significance, becoming vital as a means of reassuring herself that her existence had both usefulness and meaning.

She was born at a time when women were denied the right to vote and were considered to be quite literally the property of their husbands, and while she had managed to free herself from many of the more pernicious assumptions concerning the role of women, she was still inclined to look at the world with the downcast eyes of a supplicant. She could not escape, either, from the yearning she had always felt to have a father, and there was something almost child-like in the way she subordinated herself to Dad — so much so, in fact, that sometimes we children tended to think of her more as a beloved older sister than as a parent, a perception which the age difference between her and Dad only served to compound. She was every bit as eager to please Dad as we were, and since her industriousness seldom failed to win his praise and admiration, hers was a compelling example indeed.

No wonder I was driven to wield the scythe and the sledgehammer, to dig and shovel and heave hay bales around until my back ached and my hands were raw and blistered. As to whether I liked the work or not, the answer is a resounding "No": I detested it, but therein lay its extraordinary potency, for if I had enjoyed it or found it easy, it would have given me no sense of accomplishment. Having been raised on a steady diet of Dad's criticism, I had become so convinced of my own incurable mediocrity that only real mortification of the flesh any longer had the power to lift the leaden sense of worthlessness which by now walked with me like my own shadow.

I brought the same stringency to my schoolwork, indenturing myself with masochistic zeal to a life of academic servitude by shunning whatever I found easy or enjoyable and focusing grimly on subjects for which I had little natural aptitude and even less liking. Inevitably, although I struggled manfully with the work, I excelled in nothing. The one time I showed any promise — in art, the one indulgence I had allowed myself, and that only because I hoped it might sit well with my architect father — Dad shot me down in flames. A painting of mine was among those chosen to be displayed at the school Speech Day, a glorified PTO meeting held each fall at the start of the new school year, and for once I felt confident that Dad would return from the meeting with something good to say about me. But no: dismissing my painting as pedestrian and unimaginative, he pointedly produced from his coat pocket a rolled-up painting done by one of my classmates which he had surreptitiously stolen from the display on the Art Room wall and brought home to keep. He had the painting framed, and for years it hung in the living room at World's End, a daily reminder to me of my glaring inadequacy.

My report cards, memorable for their mediocrity, were a regular agony. The year-end ones were the worst, heavy with the finality of a judicial summing-up. They would be handed out on the last day of the summer term, and I would scarcely be able to muster the courage to look at the grades I had been given, or to read the astringent comments of my teachers, who, of course, knew nothing of the difficulties their pathologically cheerful student faced, nor could ever have imagined the firestorm of recrimination and disparagement their remarks would cause to be unleashed upon her when she got home. And while my classmates scrambled exuberantly for the exit when the final school bell of the year had sounded, I would climb slowly aboard the bus for the long ride to Hawkesworth, silent and sick with dread.

The onslaught would begin the second Dad had read the report, and would continue unabated throughout the following day: a continuous, withering commentary, complete with exhaustive lists of the manifold ways in which I had failed not only him but the entire family. Then came the statutory period of ostracism, paradoxically comforting, in its way: after such a relentless verbal assault the frozen silence came as a blessed relief. But still it wasn't over. The report card had to be signed by both parents and returned to the school at the start of the next term, and Dad pointedly refused to sign it until the night before school resumed, thereby ensuring that I would have to present him with the incriminating document once again, at the tail end of the summer vacation. And when I did so, of course, his ire would burst back to life and the haranguing would start again with renewed vigor.

I do not recall Mama ever participating actively in these ritual browbeatings. She was always there, of course, because her presence was required by Dad, but it was perfectly clear that she found the whole thing acutely unpleasant and wished it were over. She scarcely ever passed any comment when I brought my report card to her to be signed before returning it to the school, other than to ask me rather plaintively if I would please try a little harder, for her sake as well as my own, so that next time Dad might be less disappointed in me.

Not that she encouraged or condoned mediocrity. On the contrary; it was she, even more than Dad, who drummed into me the principle that one should excel in whatever one did, and that women had a particular obligation in this respect since they, on the whole, had to work twice as hard as any man to advance half as far — and she, having been one of the first women ever to gain admission to the architectural profession, knew what she was talking about. She told me once that her idea of humiliation would be to be asked

the question "What is your occupation?" and to be forced
to answer, faute de mieux, "Housewife." Fortunately, since
she had taught herself and gained qualifications in both
draftsmanship and quantity surveying, that unhappy situation never arose to trouble her. Of course she could also
have cited her prodigious talent as a linguist. Not only did
she speak the Queen's English in the most lyrical and articulate way, but she had also taught herself French, Russian and Italian, and spoke them all fluently. But even in her
domestic role she shone: she was a superb cook, a wonderful gardener, a talented seamstress and a paragon of re-
sourcefulness. When rooms needed painting, she did it;
when windows needed reglazing, she did it; when drains got
blocked, she unblocked them, plunging her arm into the
stinking mess with absolute sang froid and refusing to be
stymied by anything, however disgusting or difficult. She
brought the same level-headedness and versatility to her
work on the farm, staying up all night with farrowing sows
and helping them to deliver their enormous litters with a
compassion and patience which only someone as delighted
by babies and as experienced in the travails of childbirth as
she was could possibly have summoned. She was, in short,
an extraordinary woman, and one whose many accomplish-
ments were belied by her modest and unassuming demeanor.

She was beautiful, too: tall and slender, effortlessly and
unself-consciously elegant, even in her muddy farm
clothes. She had gray-green eyes and a wild head of hair
which had once been brown, but which, by the time I was of
an age to notice such things, had changed its mind and

begun to go gray in leaps and bounds. Although she set little store by her own appearance and was scornful of conventional prescriptions concerning feminine beauty, Dad
had other ideas. Mama's appearance was always of great importance to him. He studied her as though she were a work
in progress, and wore her beauty like a medal. Her bedroom
closet was full of shoes with preposterously high heels
which he had bought for her, and it was a source of great regret to him (although probably of profound relief to her)
when her orthopedist prohibited her, on account of her back
problems, from wearing anything but the flattest of footwear.
Dad insisted, too, that she wear lipstick at all times, his
preferred shade being a strident and uncompromising fire-
engine red. If for some reason she forgot to apply it, or if
the previous application had smudged or faded, he would
draw her attention to the fact, and she would drop whatever
she happened to be doing at once, go to the mirror and dutifully paint her lips for him. In his inimitable way he would
couch these reminders in some witty or oblique remark,
laughing mischievously as he did so. "The outlook is very
BLEAK from where I'm sitting" was a favorite, as was his
trick of pulling off a shoe and holding the sole up to Mama's
face, saying "Look at yourself, Mama!"

Wickedly funny though his comments were, and good-
humoredly though Mama always took them, they troubled
me nevertheless. It seemed so grossly unfair that Dad
should sit in judgment over Mama's appearance when she
would never have dreamed of commenting on his, even
though, to my jaundiced young eye at least, he was certainly no Adonis. It galled me, too, that Dad should see

Mama as somehow less than perfect, that he should feel
she needed improving, and that all her gentleness and
courage, her vigor and intellect counted for little if she
wasn't wearing lipstick. But I had noticed that wherever
women were concerned, their appearance was conspicuously important to Dad. Whether she was a hotel recep-
tionist or a professor of nuclear physics, a woman's looks
were invariably the object of his scrutiny and the subject of
his commentary. He had no shame about this; indeed, he
seemed to have a sense of entitlement to examine women
in this way, and to grade them on their aesthetic merits or
lack thereof. But although it used to mortify me and make
me seethe with silent rage when he admired women other
than Mama, she herself seemed cheerfully resigned to it,
just as she was to the idea that she needed lipstick in order
to be acceptable to him.

The truth is, she loved him so much, so completely and
so uncritically that she would have done anything — anything at all — to please him. So utterly dependent on his
love was she that her only real fear in life was that she might
outlive him, and given the age difference between them this
was a possibility which loomed darkly over her. Many, many
times she confided this fear to me, and, I'm sure, to Sasha
and Steve as well. She once told me that she wanted to die
with Dad, instantaneously, in a plane crash or a car wreck,
perhaps, so that they would never have to be without each
other, and I remember wondering with deep alarm how the
three of us children would ever cope with our sudden or-
phanhood. It was clear to me from a very young age that the
most important thing in Mama's life was Dad, and that how-

ever much she loved us — and she did, enormously — still her love for Dad surpassed everything else.

How lucky we all were to be loved by such a woman; what a precious gift she was to us all! Every day of my life she makes me laugh, as odd little snatches of poetry or favorite quotations of hers pop suddenly into my head for no apparent reason — much the same way, in fact, that they seemed to into hers. She'd be sitting at the kitchen table drinking her first, steaming hot cup of coffee of the day, when she'd say:

> *Full many a man, both young and old,*
> *Has come to his sarcophagus*
> *By pouring boiling coffee*
> *Down his cold esophagus.*

Or she'd glance out the window, notice it was raining, and say, absentmindedly:

> *The rain it raineth every day*
> *Upon the just and unjust fella;*
> *But more upon the just because*
> *The unjust steals the just's umbrella.*

She'd get an itch in the middle of her back, and, unable to reach it, she'd remark, "God bless the Duke of Argyll, who set up posts for the Itch." Or she'd hear someone's tummy rumbling, and would say:

I sat next to the Duchess at tea;
It was just as I thought it would be.
Her rumblings abdominal
Were something phenomenal,
And everyone thought it was me.

There wasn't always a reason or a relevance. These things would just arrive in her consciousness, and she would recite them, apropos of nothing in particular:

How odd of God
To choose the Jews.
But then the goyim
Annoy 'im.

And then, maybe:

The stinking goat on yonder hill
Feeds all day on chlorophyll.

Sometimes her quotations were purposeful, though, and designed to make a point, which they did, memorably:

"God's on our side!"
"Gott mit uns!"
The embattled nations shout.
"My God!" said God;
"I'll have my work cut out!"

Or:

> *One cannot hope to bribe or twist,*
> *Thank God, the British journalist;*
> *But seeing what the man'll do unbribed,*
> *There's no occasion to.*

She particularly loved Hilaire Belloc's *Cautionary Tales* —
and so did we, never tiring of hearing her recount the stories of willful children and the terrible fates which befell
them:

> *Matilda told such dreadful lies,*
> *It made one gasp and stretch one's eyes;*
> *Her aunt, who, from her earliest youth,*
> *Had kept a strict regard for truth,*
> *Attempted to believe Matilda:*
> *The effort very nearly killed her.*

Her memory for poetry and classical quotations was astonishing. She knew the origin of every obscure couplet imaginable, and could usually recite the whole poem which
went with it. She knew Shakespeare and Keats and Milton
and Wordsworth; Donne and Byron and Shelley and Ten-
nyson and innumerable other poets and authors, lesser and
greater, serious and funny, ancient and modern, English,
French, Russian and American, and quoted them all with
equal ease, delight and spontaneity. And often — very
often — she quoted from the Bible, for she was above all a
person of principle, a profoundly moral person, and to her
the Bible was one long, passionate poem about ethics, social justice and human dignity. Her belief was quite simply

that Jesus was the first real revolutionary, and that he was
executed because all his talk about the meek inheriting the
earth and blessed are the poor represented a serious threat
to the imperial Roman status quo.

There were very few things which disturbed Mama's
equanimity or made her truly angry, but racism and fas-
cism were two of them — or one, really, since in this murderous century they have so often been seen walking hand
in hand. Mama despised the Afrikaaner regime in South
Africa and steadfastly refused ever to buy any goods at all
from that country, something highly unusual in the England of the fifties and early sixties, and even more unusual
in the sleepy Cotswold town where Mama did her weekly
grocery shopping. Undaunted by the shopkeeper's heavy
sarcasm and obvious irritation at her questioning of the
pedigree of every item in his store, she persisted doggedly
in her boycott, and took every opportunity to inform the
shopkeeper and anyone else within earshot of the exact
reason why. I remember how she reacted when the news of
the Sharpeville massacre was broadcast over BBC radio:
she cried with rage and shame, thumping the kitchen table
with her clenched fist in bitter frustration, her face set in a
scowl of loathing for the Afrikaaner butchers who had done
this terrible thing.

That same terrifying look of incandescent hatred, so absolutely unlike the smiling, tenderhearted, forgiving Mama
I knew, crossed her face on another occasion which sticks
in my mind. We were in the cinema, and, as was usual in
those days, a short newsreel was shown before the main
feature. This particular newsreel contained footage from

the Second World War, including scenes from the liberation of Buchenwald and the burning of the Warsaw ghetto. She suddenly took my hand in the darkness and squeezed it so hard it hurt me. She was torn, I am sure, between the longing to protect me from exposure to the unspeakable ghastliness and horror on the screen, and the determination to kindle in me the same sense of passionate outrage which she herself felt.

The outrage won, and I am forever grateful. Her gifts to me have been innumerable. Most of them have brought me happiness and laughter, comfort and peace, but there are those — and this is one of them — which have brought me pure and inconsolable sadness. And that is exactly as it should be.

Lulls in the frenzied calendar of farming are rare, but there was always a period of a few weeks after school finished for the summer, and before the barley and wheat were ready to be harvested, when the farm could be left more or less to its own devices, and during this time we would take our summer vacation. Invariably that meant going across the English Channel to Europe, where we would travel from country to country, the five of us living, eating and sleeping (or trying to) at miserably close quarters, in a tiny trailer which was never intended to house more than two small and very even-tempered people.

These vacations had nothing whatever to do with relaxation. The itinerary was dictated almost entirely by architectural considerations, and we would travel vast distances

to get from one architectural masterpiece to another, sticking doggedly to a tight schedule which precluded any
dawdling. Even stopping for meals was done grudgingly,
and to the clock, and Dad would heap opprobrium on any
of us who were forced by our less than capacious bladders
to beg for a bathroom stop. Our car was the same old battered Land Rover that doubled for service on the farm: a
pickup, basically, devoid of any refinements. Mama and
Dad sat in the cab, taking turns to drive, while we children
sat where we could in the back. There was no upholstery,
nor even any seats, only the wheel arches, and with just the
canvas canopy to cover us and come between us and the
road, the engine and tire noise were overwhelming, making
conversation well-nigh impossible. Together, the noise and
the unrelieved discomfort conspired to prevent anything
more than the briefest escape into sleep. This was probably just as well, though, because Dad reserved some of his
most scathing attacks for the boorish child who chose to in-
dulge in stultifying sleep rather than stay alert and im-
prove her mind. These endless days of cramp and bruises,
dust and deafening noise, punctuated only by reverential
tours around vast Baroque palaces and dimly lit, ornate
churches induced a peculiar form of weariness and despair
in me. Philistine that I undoubtedly was — and what ten-
or eleven-year-old is not? — I could think of little else but
the joy of returning home to sleep in my own bed.

Europe was full, too, of places and things that deeply
disturbed me. Everywhere there were reminders of the war,
and Dad and Mama took great pains to point out these grim
landmarks to us, sparing us no detail of their horrifying

history. There was the wall plaque in a small Dutch town where two children had been hanged by the Nazis from a balcony as a reprisal for their parents' having harbored a Jew. The parents had been forced to witness the execution before being hanged themselves. There was the ruined church at Oradour-sur-Glâne into which nearly five hundred women and children had been herded, doused with gasoline and burned alive by the SS. A charred baby carriage still stood on the altar steps, exactly where it had been found after the massacre. A little distance away there stood the barn where two hundred of the town's menfolk had been similarly incinerated alive. And there was the eerie statue of an emaciated figure which stands alone on the shore of a quiet, clear-watered lake near Nantua in southwest France, a memorial to the thousands of Jews who were zealously rounded up by the Vichy regime and deported to their deaths in Auschwitz.

These images terrified me. They haunted my dreams — they still do — refusing to be dispelled by daylight. And long after the Renaissance palaces and Rococo interiors, the frescoes, pilasters and pediments had melted into a gilded blur in my memory, the images of Europe's brutal past stayed doggedly in focus, stark and incontrovertible, as though in some strange way, whether I liked it or not, they belonged to me.

$\mathcal{C}$ h a p t e r
9

We should have been inseparable, my brother and sister and I. We should have been comrades, confidants, united by the shared experience of being Dad's children and brimming with sympathy for one another's suffering. But not a bit of it: the intense rivalry that Dad had diligently fostered among us since our earliest youth had gradually strangled trust and turned us into strangers, eroding our ability to identify with one another and leaving us largely untroubled by one another's sorrows. Instead of solidarity when one of us was embroiled in a bitter feud with Dad, the others felt only a selfish sense of relief that at least it wasn't their turn this time. Even when he hit one of us — and that was a common occurrence — the others would shrug with a sheepish and fatalistic indifference, remembering all the times when they, too, had been hit, and knowing full well that they would be again.

We grew up locked in permanent contention with one another over a meager and fickle supply of paternal affection. There was never anywhere near enough to satisfy the emotional hunger of all three of us — and besides, Dad was incapable of giving to one of us without first of all deliberately and pointedly excluding the others, a tactic which was guaranteed to generate envy and ill will among us. Given this Darwinistic atmosphere it is hardly surprising that instead of sticking together we learned to sidle suspiciously around one another, bristling with jealousy and mutual distrust. And that made Mama all the more important to the three of us, since she was the only person in the family on whose love and constancy we could count without question.

Sasha, Steve and I were very unlike one another in character, and that only served to exacerbate our internecine struggles. The age difference among us didn't help, either. Steve was three years older than me, and Sasha an unbridgeable seven, which made her virtually an adult as far as I was concerned — and that left me with no illusions as to my place in the pecking order. I found Sasha distinctly intimidating, especially since she, borrowing a leaf from Dad's book, was inclined to subject me to merciless scrutiny, criticizing me for transgressions as disparate — and as trivial — as the size of the portions of salad I helped myself to at mealtimes (she always felt I took too much) and the way I used to clench my jaw to alleviate the discomfort I felt when I was cutting new teeth. (She hated that; "Nazi-face," she called me, and would smack my chin hard to force me to stop it.) I looked on her as almost an extension of Dad — Dad's deputy, in a way — so closely did she mirror his inquisitorial manner at times.

Like him, she seemed to feel that it was both necessary and desirable to dissect my behavior and analyze my motives as though even my thoughts and feelings were the property of the entire family. She seemed to think she knew better than I did what I thought and felt, a conceit drawn directly from Dad's arsenal — he was forever dismissing his children's opinions as blatant manifestations of the power of self-deception — and she claimed, just as Dad did, that she understood me far better than I would ever be able to understand myself.

As I look back on these things now, of course, I can see that she was just as lost and tormented, just as lonely and uncertain and starved of affection as I was. Maybe she hoped that by controlling me so closely (a technique she had learned at the knee of a master) she might manage to bring some semblance of stability into her own precarious existence. Maybe, in her own way, especially as she got older, she simply wanted to take me under her wing. Nevertheless, it seemed to me at the time that I was under attack, and in the face of such relentless intrusions it was no wonder that my fledgling sense of self took a near-mortal beating. Robbed of even the bare bones of autonomy and rendered to all intents and purposes public property, I grew up feeling naked and transparent. The small efforts I made to create oases of privacy for myself by locking my bedroom door or by going for long walks by myself only served to invite accusations of secretiveness, something profoundly disapproved of in the Lubetkin family.

I began writing poetry and keeping a diary, spending

hours alone, sitting high up among the hay bales in the old barn, and hiding my efforts behind a loose stone in the barn wall. Once, rashly, I showed a poem I'd written about cats to my English teacher at school, and he published it in the school magazine, something which earned me a spell in Dad's good books — and, therefore, made me the object of Sasha's ravening jealousy. Unable to bear the fact that I had conceived and written the poem all by myself, she accused me of having plagiarized it, and despite the fact that she could not pinpoint the source of my poem, she was nevertheless able, by citing my recent tendency toward secretiveness, to persuade Mama and Dad that I had indeed copied it, and that I was lying when I denied having done so. I distinctly remember the overwhelming feeling of abject helplessness which this incident brought about. I had done something praiseworthy, and yet here I was accused on all sides of dishonesty, and no one would listen to the truth. It seemed to me that everyone *wanted* to believe the worst of me, to find me guilty and to write me off as irredeemably worthless and duplicitous.

I still have the diary I kept in those suffocatingly kafkaesque days. There was no more than an inch of space for each daily entry, and I had to adapt my indignation and my handwriting accordingly, but even so it makes poignant and evocative reading. "Remember how sad you were today," reads one stark entry, no explanation given, none needed, even all these years later. And pasted on another page a yellowed newspaper clipping containing a quotation from Strindberg that I had cut out and kept as a talisman, a reminder that others had lived the way the Lubetkins, the

World's End fighters, lived; had suffered the same injustices and yet had survived:

Sacred family! The supposed home of all the virtues, where innocent children are tortured into their first falsehoods, where wills are broken by parental tyranny, and self-respect smothered by crowded, jostling egos.

As for Steve, he dealt with his pain very privately, rarely allowing anyone but Mama to see his true feelings. He told me once that he had realized when he was still very young that Dad didn't love him, and all Mama's impassioned assurances to the contrary had failed to disabuse him of that notion. But unrequited love has a habit of redoubling its efforts, and despite having confronted the awful reality that he was unloved, he remained as hopelessly in thrall to Dad as we all were. I vividly remember a night long, long after we had all grown up and left home, when Steve and I, both students by then, in the same city, and friends at last, sat up late talking, as students do, our conversation spurred recklessly on by chain-smoking and cheap wine. We fell to discussing the myriad hardships of our childhood at World's End, and Steve, his voice betraying the tears his handsome face had so resolutely hardened to restrain, suddenly blurted out: "Lu, we'll never be free until Dad's dead."

I said nothing at the time. What could one say, after all? These were his true feelings, the product of a lifetime's worth of rejection and dutifully repressed anger. Besides, I was still young then — twenty-two, maybe — and not much given to pondering mortality, my own or anyone else's. But even so I had my doubts about the liberating effect of Dad's death. I felt then, just as I do now, that the bonds between Dad and us were utterly indestructible — and God knows that by then I had done just about everything in my power to sever them.

There may have been little love lost between my siblings and me, but at least there was a certain statistical strength in numbers, and never was this more apparent to me than when first Sasha, and soon after that Steve, departed for college, delirious with the promise of freedom. Their going robbed me of my cover, for where Dad had previously had three targets to choose from when he felt moved to excoriate his children or enumerate their many shortcomings, now he only had one, and at fifteen I was left facing the dismal prospect of his undivided attention for a further three years before I, too, might expect release.

By now Dad was sixty-five, and what little lenience he may once have possessed had long since hardened into steely inflexibility. With little else to divert him, he began to focus on me with an unblinking intensity, policing my activities, my schoolwork and my friendships with a frightful vigilance, listening to my phone conversations, reading my letters and withholding my mail as though it were his right and his duty to know exactly what was going on in my head and my heart at all times. His paranoia even extended to insisting that I accompany him and Mama whenever they had to leave the house for a few hours to do errands, in order to prevent me from having time alone and unsupervised at home — although exactly what he imagined I might get up to all by myself out there in the sepulchral silence and isolation of Upper Killington, I cannot imagine.

A child with a history of truancy, delinquency or habitual dishonesty might perhaps expect to incur such vigorous parental control, but I had never shown any sign of being anything other than compliant, almost to the point of servility. Dad's unceasing and obsessive surveillance, his relentless fault-finding and censoriousness filled me with burning resentment. For so long I had dutifully effaced my own sense of self, stuffing pillows in its mouth, depriving it of the right to be heard, and telling it, when it did manage to get a word in edgewise, that it didn't know what it was talking about. I began to challenge Dad's authority, albeit obliquely, questioning his political convictions, drawing his attention to some of the glaring contradictions in his own position. If the West was so malevolent and the Soviet Union so marvelous, why hadn't he stayed there? Why were we living in England, not the USSR? Of course these outbursts cost me dear: Dad saw them for what they were, rebelliousness, pure and simple, and, adding political deviancy to the long list of my misdemeanors, he reacted accordingly, using them to justify ever more Draconian controls over me.

Appeals to Mama were no use. For twenty years she had been stuck in the middle, pulled this way and that, torn to shreds by conflicting loyalties. Now she stood aside, mute and downcast, unwilling any longer even to mediate, for fear of the merciless bludgeoning she would undoubtedly suffer if she were to try. Forced to choose between her husband and her youngest child, she chose her husband — her child was young and strong, after all, and she would survive. Soon she would be old enough to leave home, as Sasha and Steve already had — and they had survived, hadn't they? So would Lu. They all would. Only another year or two.

The truth is, she was just plain worn out. A terrible tiredness seemed to have overcome her, sapping her once indomitable spirit and leaving little energy to spare for endeavors as futile and dangerous as trying to rein in Dad's excesses. She laughed less and less often these days, and her encyclopedic repertoire of poems and quotations, puns and limericks fell into disuse — what was there to laugh about now, what with the constant quarreling and the frigid silences? It was this, more than anything, which alarmed me and restrained my mutinousness, for the thought that I was somehow responsible for silencing Mama's laughter made me utterly disconsolate and filled me with self-loathing.

Her health was not what it had been either. She began to notice a curious sensation of coolness, coupled with pins and needles, in her ankles and feet, and occasionally her hand shook uncontrollably as she tried to pick up a cup. She was admitted to the hospital for tests and stayed there for several days, during which time Dad and I rattled miserably around in the empty old house, our hostilities temporarily suspended in the light of the fear and alarm we both felt concerning Mama. The day before her planned homecoming, Dad returned gray-faced from visiting her, told me to sit down with him at the kitchen table and revealed that the doctors suspected Mama was in the very early stages of multiple sclerosis.

That night I slept little, and I don't think Dad even bothered going to bed. Hearing sounds coming from the kitchen in the early hours of the morning, I crept downstairs and found Dad standing at the window, watching the first glimmers of daylight breaking across the valley. His shoulders were shaking, and tears were scrambling down his crumpled cheeks like lemmings. He hadn't expected to be seen in such disarray. Sentimental though he could be, he hated displays of emotion and was always fiercely critical of me for the ease with which I could be reduced to tears. Turning away from me, he composed himself so quickly and so completely that if I hadn't known better I might really have believed that all that eye wiping and nose blowing was merely due to an attack of sneezing. I pretended I'd seen nothing untoward because it was obvious that he hated to be seen in a position of such vulnerability, but the image of him reduced to tears by the fear of losing Mama was a precious and profoundly endearing one to me, and one which I never forgot regardless of how turbulent and acrimonious our relationship subsequently became.

Mama returned home looking tired and pale, but World's End soon worked its peculiar restorative magic on her, as it always had, and although she continued to have the symptom of cold and prickly feet ("refrigerated horsehair ankle socks," she called it, dismissively, refusing to be intimidated by her doctors' diagnosis), the disease remained blessedly and mysteriously stuck in its infancy, never fulfilling its terrifying early promise.

The farm had shrunk in recent years. Most of the livestock and a substantial portion of the arable land had been sold off, and there was a great deal less work to be done now in terms of running the place. Paradoxically, though, that made World's End feel more than ever like a prison to me. Deprived of the excuse to be outdoors, and now with no pretext for escaping from the house for a few hours, I spent most of my time sitting silently in my bedroom, struggling with my schoolwork. And a struggle it was, too, for in my quest for Dad's elusive approval I had committed myself on entering Senior High to a grueling curriculum of pure sciences — subjects not for the dreamer, the easily distracted or the dilettante, all of which, by nature, I undoubtedly was.

Academic rigors notwithstanding, though, I thanked God for the small mercy of my daily parole to attend school. At least that got me away from World's End and allowed me to be with other people, people who were not constantly seeking to constrain my outlook or impose their own ideology on me. Sensing that school meant so much to me, Dad began punishing my peccadilloes by refusing to drive me to Hawkesworth to catch the school bus, or to fetch me after school at night, and I would be compelled to walk the five miles to my nearest schoolmate's house in order to beg a ride from her compassionate parents — either that, or face the awful prospect of staying at home.

With school being such a lifeline for my beleaguered psyche, the long summer vacation presented a uniquely gloomy and purgatorial prospect. So when, in the summer of my seventeenth year, I received an invitation from my German pen-friend to spend the entire month of August at her home in Bavaria, I closed my eyes and begged every conceivable deity to soften Dad's heart and make him consent to let me go. Amazingly, he did agree. Who knows why? Maybe he, too, was worn out by the endless conflict between us and relished the chance to spend a month alone with Mama at World's End, just him and her, the way things had been in those wonderful, childless early days. Whatever his reasons, I was at last being set free, and I can clearly remember the exhilaration I felt as I boarded the train at the start of that long journey, kissing my parents a joyful good-bye and promising, in my gratitude, to visit every Baroque palace within striking distance of my friend Sabine's home.

Sabine lived in the town of Prien, on the shore of Lake Chiemsee, not far from Munich. She and her family spent a lot of time sailing on the lake, which was certainly a complete change for a lifelong landlubber like me; but very soon I tired of sailing, and, giddy with my newfound sense of independence, I longed to go off on my own and explore. One afternoon, while Sabine and her family were out sailing on the lake as usual, I opted instead to borrow her bicycle and go for a ride into the town by myself. I didn't tell Sabine this, of course, but I had never ridden a bicycle before, and moreover, coming as I did from one of the most sparsely populated areas of rural England, I was entirely unused to traffic, especially traffic which drove on the right. Meandering wildly, I provoked yells of annoyance and remonstration from passing motorists. I tried to keep as far to the right as I could to enable cars to pass me uneventfully, but soon found myself wobbling dangerously, and before I knew what had happened, I had plowed into a parked car, plunging my hand clean through the side-view mirror.

Passersby began gathering around me at once, clucking over my badly mangled hand, which was now bleeding enthusiastically; but my immediate worries were more for Sabine's crumpled bicycle and the scratched and dented car I'd hit than for the injury I'd inflicted on myself. Who would pay for the damage I'd done? How would I explain what had happened to the owner of the car, or to Sabine's parents? I was in trouble, no doubt about it; and as I sat there fretting on the sidewalk, a dozen anxious citizens of Prien fussing over the young *Engländerin* with the badly bleeding hand, I was struck by the irony of the fact that here I was, really on my own for the first time in my life, yet what I wanted most in all the world was for Mama and Dad to be there to help me.

A taxi took me to a local hospital, a grim place, as they all are. The hospital was staffed by an order of Carmelite nuns in full traditional habits, including starched headdresses so elaborately folded and so wide that there was not room for two to pass each other in the dismal, paneled hallway. I was bleeding impressively by now, and without further ado I was ushered into a small operatory where a doctor was waiting for me.

He was in his middle to late fifties, a gray-haired, bespectacled man with a stiff and unsmiling demeanor. He wore a long green rubber apron which reminded me vividly of the one the veterinarian wore when attending to the obstetrical needs of the World's End cattle. The nuns must have told him that I was English, for he spoke to me with the slow, exaggerated elocution that people use when addressing idiots and foreigners. He seemed particularly interested in my name. "Lubetkin," he said. "Lubetkin. What sort of a name is that?" "Russian," I replied. "My father came from Russia." "Oh?" he returned. "But Lubetkin is a Jewish name. Are you Jewish?" "No," I replied, wondering whether I should even try to embark upon the convoluted saga of Dad and his assumed name. I wasn't at all sure my very basic German could be stretched to cover such a long and involved story, and besides, I was beginning to feel distinctly faint with shock and fear. If this was the doctor's attempt at polite conversation, if he was trying to put me at my ease, he had failed miserably. There was something profoundly disturbing about him, and I was immensely thankful for the presence of the nun-nurse in her starched butterfly headdress.

And then the doctor set to work. Stretching my hand out on a stainless steel table, he took a hard-bristled nailbrush and began scrubbing the ragged wounds with an unnatural zeal — and since he had not seen fit to bother with niceties such as local anesthesia, the pain was excruciating. There was no anesthesia, either, for the eighteen stitches it took to close all the wounds. I lay there, face averted, biting my lip so hard that it bled, conjuring up images of my beloved

Mama, who set such store by bravery and dignity, and I fought with all my might to do her justice by not crying.

The doctor stood up and, after dismissing the nun from the room, told me he would now give me antitetanus shots. In England nearly all shots are given in the upper arm, so I pushed back the sleeve of my T-shirt as best I could for him. He stopped me. "No," he said. "Take off your clothes." I did as he said. With his face wearing the expressionless mask of clinical detachment, and with his hand unshaken by shame or compassion, he administered a tetanus shot with studious precision into the nipple of both my breasts. Then, without a word, he turned on his heel and left the room. A short while later, the nun returned and told me I could go.

I went home to England a couple of days later, my month of freedom abruptly at an end. The incident had laid me so low that my hosts became worried and called Mama and Dad to tell them that they were putting me on a plane for London.

I wasn't really sure how Mama and Dad would react. I was prepared for outrage and indignation toward that doctor, whose vile agenda had been so clearly visible in the questions he had asked about my name, and the cruel, perverted way he had treated me. I was even prepared for anger: after all, I should never have taken such a risk, especially not all alone, in a foreign country, unused as I was to traffic. What I wasn't prepared for was indifference — and that is exactly what I got.

Neither Mama nor Dad showed the slightest surprise or resentment toward the doctor. On the contrary, they dismissed the questions he had asked me as being perfectly innocent — simply a natural curiosity on his part, they said, concerning a patient with an unusual name. They told me I was being hysterical and melodramatic when I suggested that he might be a former Nazi bent on humiliating me because he thought I was Jewish. And as for the injections in my breasts, well, they did things differently on the Continent. Sometimes they gave shots in one's behind, Mama said, and sometimes in other parts; just different customs, that's all. Nothing to worry about. He must have had good reason to choose that particular technique.

I was devastated by their reaction. I had been through something savage and unspeakable, and there they were telling me I was making a mountain out of a molehill, that nothing untoward had happened, and that I was the one with the problem. I could not accept it. Surely I was worth more than that? I felt abandoned — and worse, violated all over again, this time by my own parents — and I told them exactly that.

The result was predictable. Whipping his glasses off, Dad leaped to his feet and glared at me, his face suddenly suffused with rage. "You will take that remark back and apologize for it immediately!" he roared. "No, I won't," I replied, strangely calm, and full of an unfamiliar sensation of self-assurance. "I meant every word."

The force of the blow Dad struck me sent me reeling to the floor. I got up slowly, my head spinning and my ears humming. Mama was sitting at the kitchen table, her head in her hands, sobbing. "Get out!" Dad shouted at me. "Okay," I said. And that night, taking only the clothes I stood up in, and the little money I had in my purse, I left World's End forever.

Part Two

∾

Hunger

C h a p t e r
1 0

໑໑ When Helen Coombs glanced through her open kitchen window and saw me walking purposefully up her driveway she was not altogether surprised. In the last few months before my abrupt departure from World's End I had sought her help with increasing frequency, turning up on her doorstep and begging rides to school after walking the five miles from Upper Killington when Dad had refused to drive me to Hawkesworth to catch the school bus. Her daughter Susie, a classmate of mine and my only really close friend, knew a great deal about the tribulations I faced, and from what Susie had told her she knew that things between Dad and me had been going from bad to worse, and that it was only a matter of time before a crisis erupted.

Now here I was, fresh from my final confrontation with Dad, my face still flushed and smarting from his blow, my mind still racing like floodwater, churning and roiling with all the bitter things I wished I had said to him. Stalwart that she was, Mrs. Coombs sat me down at the kitchen table, put a large mug of coffee in front of me, and listened.

This was an unnatural experience for me. I had become so used to having to explain myself, justify myself, demonstrate loyalty to my family by seeking their approval for everything I did that I no longer expected to be listened to, still less to be heard, understood and believed. Yet here was Mrs. Coombs taking me at my word, neither judging, nor challenging, nor overruling me, simply wanting to know what had happened, what I'd like to do now and how she could help me.

I told her far more than she could ever conceivably have wanted to know about what had happened. I told her that what I wanted to do now was to live my own life, find my own way and answer to no one but myself. And I asked her if I could stay with her and Susie for a short while, just until I found my feet. I had a place at university for the following academic year, and a generous state grant to fund me, so that if my parents decided to punish me by withdrawing financial support I would still have my tuition and basic living expenses paid. What I needed more than anything was a peaceful place I could think of as home until it was time for me to leave for university. And so I stayed out the year with the kindly Coombs family, who treated me like their own daughter, sheltered me and fed me and gave me comfort, and refused to take any money whatever from me by way of rent.

Of course my parents guessed where I had gone, and telephoned Mrs. Coombs soon after my departure from World's End to confirm their suspicions. Mrs. Coombs maintained a studious neutrality, shunning discussion of rights and wrongs and quietly reassuring my parents that I was safe, and that I planned to work for the next few months before leaving for university. It staggered her that Mama declined her offer to fetch me to the phone — but it didn't surprise me one bit. I knew Mama was obeying Dad's orders. Sasha, however, who had left World's End a full seven years earlier, and was now happily married and living in London, clearly felt that ostracism was not the best way to deal with my lone rebellion. She wasted no time in writing to me and commanding me to return home at once. Her furious letter berated me for my disloyalty in involving outsiders in family matters, described me as shallow and stupendously selfish, and laid the responsibility for Mama's well-being squarely at my door. If I did not return home immediately, she said, any decline in Mama's health would be entirely attributable to me, and no one in the family would ever forgive me for what I had done.

This was not the first time in my life that Sasha had taken it upon herself to act as whipper-in, nor would it be the last — that's the duty, after all, of an older sister — but even so the sheer unfairness of her outburst staggered me. Why was she so inordinately willing to see the worst in me? Why had she accepted so uncritically the version of events which Dad had fed her? Had she forgotten the bitter experience of her own childhood? How could she have let fly at me with both barrels in this way, as though I, and I alone, were the source of all the strife that had riven the Lubetkin family throughout the years?

The strong, secure, self-confident recipient of such a

letter might well have been sufficiently dismayed by the
contents and upset by the hectoring tone to have replied in
kind. But I was far from strong. Then not quite eighteen, I
was the youngest member of a deeply troubled family, and
the last to pass through the protracted ordeal of a Lubetkin
childhood. I had certainly learned endurance, but endurance is not strength; strength comes from fortitude and
an inner conviction that one can and will overcome adver-
sity, and I had no such belief. I was driven only by the
stolid, unreasoning impetus of my will to survive, a blind
momentum which told me that I had no choice but to leave,
that I could only become myself once I had torn free of my
family.

Neither was I secure and self-confident. As I saw it, I
had no reason to believe in myself or to feel confident of
my abilities — the very opposite, in fact. Since infancy my
shortcomings had been relentlessly pointed out to me,
while my triumphs had gone generally unremarked. On the
few occasions when I had come top of my class Dad had
brushed my success aside, remarking that the teachers had
obviously graded my work too leniently, or that the school's
standards were so abysmally low that even dullards shone.
I was now so unshakably convinced of my own mediocrity
that I neither liked myself nor could believe that others
might like me — and if they appeared to like me it could
only be because they had been hoodwinked by my outward
persona. Had they been able to see the real me, the unlovable, worthless creature so well known to my family, they
would undoubtedly have changed their minds and walked
hurriedly away from me. At heart I felt like a fraud, an im-

postor. Even Susie, I was sure, wouldn't want me as a friend if she found out how inferior I truly was. And it therefore came as no surprise to me that my own sister, who had always claimed that she could see right through me, found me so abhorrent that she felt impelled to write and tell me as much.

Maybe Sasha's right, I thought. Maybe I am to blame for Mama's ill health. Certainly I'm the cause of her current unhappiness, and who knows? Maybe she might never have developed MS in the first place if it hadn't been for the constant friction between Dad and me these past few years. Maybe I should go home, apologize to Dad for her sake (Though for what? Simply for being?) and beg his forgiveness? But tormented though I was with guilt and self-doubt, I knew I had crossed the Rubicon. I did not want to return to the fold, to surrender myself once more to the intrusions and psychological trespassing that had made my childhood such hell. The price of making peace with my family would be the surrender of the precious autonomy I had won, and I would be drawn back into that dismal, powerless orbit again, to circulate only as far and as fast as permitted by Dad. No matter what, I was not going back.

Nevertheless, I missed Mama enormously, and hated the feeling of being cut off from her. And cut off I was: Dad had forbidden her to see me, to write to me or to speak to me on the phone. For several months after I left home I had no contact with her at all. But once I reached university I felt emboldened by the physical distance that now separated me from World's End, and I wrote to Mama — knowing full well that Dad would intercept the letter and read it first — asking if I might perhaps be allowed to speak to her from time to time by phone. I proposed a date and time for my first call, and, having heard nothing from her to suggest that she would refuse to speak to me, I plucked up courage and dialed the number.

The phone rang for a long time, and I could clearly picture the scene in the smoky kitchen at World's End as the insistent ringing pulled Mama one way and Dad's thunderous silence and censorious glare pulled her the other. Eventually, though, he must have nodded assent, for she picked up the phone and answered, the way she always did, "Doddington 251?," not giving her name but instead saying the phone number in the form of a question, as though she were sure that the person who was calling must have made a mistake, and couldn't possibly have intended to seek out the Lubetkins in their secret world. But of course this time she knew perfectly well who was calling, and despite the frostiness in her voice, and the unmistakable sound of Dad breathing angrily and smothering a cough as he eavesdropped on our conversation from the phone in the bedroom, a precedent had been established.

I phoned her regularly after that, but our conversations were always painfully awkward, even though we stuck firmly to pleasantries and factual matters, never venturing into discussions about the rift. At first I attributed this to the fact that Dad was invariably listening in, but on the rare occasions when I caught her alone at home, her voice still carried that note of terseness and reproach which let me know in no uncertain terms that she did not feel comfortable talking to me at all. She seemed to be inhibited by her own exaggerated sense of loyalty to Dad, as though even talking to me at all were a betrayal, a seditious act against him. Mama had always been the sole source of love and comfort in my life, and I could not bear to sever all contact with her, especially not now, when I was in a completely unfamiliar environment, struggling to make decisions and to direct my own life, with no one to turn to for help. And I was facing some hard realities too.

The English education system at that time was dedicated to a policy of early specialization. Sciences and arts were considered on the whole to be immiscible and mutually exclusive, and students in their last few years of high school were required to make a choice between the two, a decision that carried enormous consequences in terms of what careers would later be open to them. My proclivity for picking the subjects which I found most taxing and rigorous had led me inexorably toward the sciences — which also, conveniently, happened to be the subjects most venerated by Dad — and when the time came for me to apply to universities, all of which selected students on the basis of their high school specialization, my options were limited. I finally settled on the idea of studying pharmacy. I had really wanted to study medicine, since medicine was just about the only profession for which Dad had any respect, and I felt sure that if I could become a doctor I would stand a good chance of earning myself a stable and permanent place in his good books. However, I knew I would never be able to achieve the perfect grades necessary to gain admission to medical school, and as it turned out I was right. I scraped through my final exams with grades only just high enough to secure me the place I had been provisionally offered at the school of pharmacy — and even that, I thought, was a minor miracle.

Once I got there, of course, I found myself faced with formidable new hurdles. University-level science was infinitely more difficult than the science I had been exposed to in high school — and heaven knows I had had enough trouble mastering that. Now it was no longer adequate merely to memorize facts and cram one's head with formulae and principles as though for a catechism. One was expected to think like a scientist, to have a gymnastic ability with math, and, for pharmacy students in particular, to feel entirely at home in the honeycomb world of organic chemistry, with its methyls and ethyls, its benzenes and amines, each sprawling molecule more anonymous and inscrutable than the last. I was hopelessly out of my depth, and I knew it could only get worse.

For so long I had been fighting my natural inclinations, shunning the things I found absorbing and interesting in favor of those with which I had to wrestle every inch of the way. I had thought that by lacing myself with grim determination into the harshest and most restrictive intellectual corset I could find I would become living proof of Dad's dictum that the concept of natural ability, like that of human nature, was entirely fictitious — the former being useful only to rationalize laziness, and the latter to justify the iniquities of the status quo. Self-discipline was all that was needed, he said: concentration, *Sitzfleisch*, strength of character. Nothing one finds easy is ever worthwhile; only those things which require a struggle have any value.

But far from triumphing over my own laziness and proving the infinite adaptability of the human intellect, all I had really done was to maroon myself without any immediate hope of rescue. Universities in those days tended to be even more rigidly compartmentalized than the schools: there was no provision for students like me, who felt they had boarded the wrong train years before and wanted to go back and find the right one. Places — and grants — were awarded to read for specific degrees, and if a student had left school with a record of specialization in pure sciences, then pure sciences — or, at a pinch, applied sciences, like pharmacy — were all that were open to her. For better or for worse, science and I were stuck with each other, and the best I could do was to try to find some other subject — physiology, maybe, or zoology — within the science faculty which might involve less math and chemistry, and might therefore be a bit more manageable.

I had not wanted any hint of my difficulties to reach Dad, and took pains, whenever Mama and I spoke on the phone, to avoid the subject of my studies, brushing her questions aside breezily or giving noncommittal answers. Why should I hand Dad the stick to beat me with, I thought; he'll be delighted that I'm struggling, and will jump at the chance to remind Mama of how he'd told her all along that I was intellectually inferior and that I had no staying power. But with our phone conversations already so stiff and tense, my reluctance to talk about such a seemingly neutral subject as my studies must have struck Mama — and, of course, Dad, who was always stealthily listening in — as very suspicious, and I might have known that they

would not allow it to pass. Nevertheless, I hadn't anticipated the lengths to which they would go to try to prevent
me from exercising my fledgling autonomy.

Not long after I had begun the process of transferring to
the physiology degree course, Mama, acting on Dad's orders, called the head of the school of pharmacy and asked
to know how my studies were going. Then, of course, the
full story of my proposed transfer emerged, and before the
week was out I was summoned to the Dean's office and
handed a letter that he had received from Dad. Similar letters, he said, had also been received at the school of pharmacy and the school of physiology — and also, for reasons
he was powerless to fathom (and considerably too diplomatic), by the head of my hall of residence. The letter had
been typed by Mama, but the wording, the tone and the
nakedly punitive intent were pure Dad:

Dear Dean,

*We were dismayed to discover that our daughter, Louise, who
scraped into the university only by the skin of her teeth, has already disgraced herself academically — but we were not at all
surprised. Since early childhood Louise has exhibited an alarming inability to concentrate, a half-hearted and dilatory approach
to schoolwork and an absolute lack of self-discipline.*

*That she should have shown her true colors so soon after start-
ing her university career surely demonstrates with unequivocal finality that she is not only incapable of applying herself, but also
that she is inadequately endowed intellectually to cope with anything more strenuous than a vocational or clerical career — secretarial work, say, or at most nursing. It is our considered opinion*

that by allowing her to abandon the pharmacy degree course we would not only be encouraging her dilettantism, but would also be guilty of a profligate wastage of public money, since her tuition and fees are government funded.

It is our firm belief that Louise should be compelled either to continue in the school of pharmacy or to withdraw entirely from the university, ceding her place to a worthier candidate, and we intend to do all in our power to ensure that these are the only two options made available to her. Our concern is for the welfare of our daughter, and we would be failing miserably in our duty as parents if we allowed her irresponsible and aimless wandering to continue.

Yours truly,

Berthold and Margaret Lubetkin

What choice was there? The university, the Dean said, would support any decision I made, and if I still wanted to transfer to physiology they would put no obstacles in my path. However, he said, it was clear that my parents, for reasons best known to themselves, were vehemently opposed to the idea. Was I ready to fight for transfer to a course which it was by no means certain that I would find any more agreeable? What would happen if my parents succeeded in getting my student grant revoked, which well they might? Why didn't I just try to finish the year in pharmacy, and then we could all sit down and reassess the situation? Maybe by then, he added, my parents' antagonistic attitude might have mellowed somewhat, and the atmosphere might be more conducive to compromise.

Yet again, my parents were treating me like a puppet, speaking for me, talking over my head, discussing me — and in the most devastatingly cruel and derogatory terms — as though I were not there and had no life, no mind of my own. And the worst thing was that I really had little choice but to bow to their wishes. Rather than quit the university and end up all alone in a strange city with no money, no job and nowhere to live, I decided to stick with pharmacy until the end of the academic year.

My anger and resentment reached such heights that I went to a lawyer and began proceedings to change my name by deed poll from Lubetkin to Whittaker. Why Whittaker? No reason in particular except that it sounded so thoroughly unremarkable, so neutral and so unquestionably English. And the name Lubetkin was by now absolute anathema to me, representing as it did my connection to Dad, and to a family which seemed prepared to accept me only on condition that I relinquish control of my life and cede it unconditionally to them. It didn't matter to me that Lubetkin was not Dad's real name: it was the flag he had sailed under since before I was born, and I felt marked by it.

But the name change was never finalized — at least, not to Whittaker. Soon after the showdown over my attempt to abandon pharmacy, I met an engineering student, then in his final year, who was as infatuated with me as I was with him. I might not be permitted to choose for myself what subject to study for a bachelor's degree, but I was now old enough, in the eyes of the law at least, to accept a proposal of marriage without needing my parents' consent. And that is exactly what I did. In the spring of my nineteenth year I married Jim, assumed his blessedly anonymous and un-prepossessing name, and quietly resigned from the university, leaving the Scylla of pharmacy and the Charybdis of physiology to heave a collective sigh of relief at my going.

"Marry in haste, repent at leisure," Mama had always said, and I quickly came to wish I had heeded her. Of course the marriage did not last; how could it have? I had jumped into it like a fugitive leaping aboard a moving train: quick, quick, there's no time to lose; what does it matter where the train is bound? The important thing is that it's going somewhere, somewhere far away, somewhere safe. I needed to escape from my family and from the imminent certainty of academic disgrace, and marriage seemed like the perfect answer. And for his part Jim, who had little respect for women in general, and even less for those who didn't respect themselves, had no idea whom he was marrying. I was a simulacrum, not a whole person; someone who seemed animated and substantial, to be sure, but who, in reality, was as incomplete and unformed as a single, stone-cold egg in an abandoned bird's nest. It was not long before it became obvious to both of us that we had made a gigantic mistake, and we parted.

Nevertheless, brief though the marriage was, and bitterly unhappy, for the short time it lasted it did indeed provide me with a haven of sorts, and gave me the chance to take my first tentative steps toward independence. I enrolled in an intensive secretarial course, learned to type and do shorthand, and began working as a secretary in the same city where I had so recently begun my abortive career in pharmacy. The work itself was extremely dull and repetitive, but at least I was on top of it and could do it well, however menial it was — and that was a new departure for me after all the years of martyring myself with science and foundering ignominiously despite my best efforts. I was even earning enough to support myself in modest comfort. But self-sufficient or not, the truth was that emotionally I was still firmly stuck in childhood, and, like any child, I longed for the love and support of my parents.

My letters and phone calls to Mama must have conveyed something of this subliminal ache, for our conversations grew longer and markedly less awkward, even though Dad, who still refused to speak to me, was always invisibly present, like an irascible, eavesdropping ghost at the feast. As time went by — and it was now more than two years since I had left World's End — the tone of reproach in her voice gave way to one of undisguised sorrow. It was clear that she desperately wanted there to be a reconciliation between me and Dad, and in the end, unable to bear the weight of her sadness on my conscience, I capitulated.

We met on neutral ground, at an Italian restaurant in London. I had gone to the meeting bristling with defensiveness and full of trepidation, certain that I was about to be subjected to the awful, familiar ritual of inquisition and appeasement, forced recantation and feigned contrition. Anxiety had painted my cheeks a fiery red, stolen my appetite and left my mouth bone dry, but the attack I had anticipated and braced myself to resist simply never arrived. There was no postmortem, no long philippic — no mention, even, of the schism which had kept us apart for so long. And even though, as always, he monopolized the conversation entirely, bolting his food and talking with his mouth full so as not to allow the mechanical business of eating to get in the way of what he had to say, still he was extraordinarily restrained — almost solicitous, even. He seemed a great deal more interested in the practical details of my life — how I was managing financially, what my flat was like — than in passing judgment on me, and I was struck by the irony of the situation. After all, never had Dad had a more cast-iron case nor a more legitimate reason to carp at me — I was not yet twenty-one and already had a failed marriage and an abandoned degree to my name — yet, paradoxically, never had he seemed less inclined to do so. Indeed, for the first time in my life I thought I detected a glimmer of something vaguely resembling respect in his attitude toward me.

Things had not been easy for them, either. Dad was now seventy, and Mama, although still in her early fifties, looked considerably older. Her hair had gone completely white, and her face, statutory scarlet lipstick notwithstanding, looked pale and gaunt. Her multiple sclerosis, whose harbingers had struck such fear into all of us a few years earlier, had remained mercifully in abeyance: she still had horsehair ankle socks, she said, but was otherwise perfectly intact. But for all her bravado Mama seemed a great deal more frail than I remembered her. Sasha's letter came back to me, as it so often had, and I looked at the change in Mama and was overcome with a terrible sense of shame for the pain my mutiny must have caused her.

There were changes afoot, too, in their lives. The demands of the farm had long since become too much for them, and they had got rid of the remaining livestock and sold off the last of the land to neighboring farmers. But even then there was the old house itself, with its drafts and leaks and recalcitrant drains, its precipitous staircase and its wild and rampant garden. It had become an intolerable burden on their dwindling finances and diminished stamina, and they had come to the conclusion that they had little choice but to sell World's End and move. Because of their advancing years and Mama's potentially frail health, they had decided to make a virtue of necessity by moving to the city, and in fact, Dad said, they had already bought a tiny, dilapidated row house and were busily organizing its renovation. World's End was on the market now, and they had been made a good offer for it. If everything went according to plan they would move to the city before the end of the year.

The news dumbfounded me. World's End had been everything to them. For as long as they had known each other it had been their nest, their retreat, their beautiful private world. Their whole life together had been built in it and around it; all their memories were there. That Mama was even prepared to countenance leaving that precious place said more about how weary and defeated she felt than she herself would ever have been prepared to admit, and again I was racked with guilt and shame for the part I had played in bringing her to this point. I swore to myself that somehow or other I would make it up to her, that one day I would do something to make her and Dad proud of me, put a feather in their cap for all time.

I had thought that by exiling myself from my family I would finally manage to break the shackles of my childhood and set myself free, but suddenly that freedom seemed like a frozen and echoing wilderness. Scientist or secretary, married or divorced, I was a child again, a little Lubetkin, a prodigal daughter who'd come home at last, and all I needed now was some way to make amends, to prove myself worthy of my parents' love. If you want me to, I will.

Not long after our reunion, Mama and Dad left World's End and moved, just as they had planned, into their little row house in a bustling city neighborhood, a stone's throw from dozens of interesting shops and restaurants. They had redesigned the house to make the ground floor into their living quarters and the upstairs a separate, self-contained flat which they intended to rent out to students. The ground floor was tiny: a single ten-foot by twelve-foot bedroom connected by a galley kitchen to a similarly modest-sized living room. French windows in the bedroom led out into a small, walled courtyard which Mama lost no time in transforming into a thronged and cheerful garden. Indeed, the first thing she did when they moved in was to plant ceremonially a generous clump of wild miniature daffodils that she had dug up and brought with her from the old orchard at World's End. The house had no name, no drama, no singular personality; it was known simply as 113, which was its street number, and that suited it perfectly.

They had laid out their flat with the possibility of a reemergence of Mama's multiple sclerosis very much in mind. All the rooms were wired for bells; there were no doors, no steps, and all the doorways were widened in order to allow a wheelchair to pass comfortably through them. But the disease confounded everyone, vanishing in petulant defiance of all the elaborate preparations which had been made to accommodate it. In fact, both Mama and Dad seemed to thrive — although it never ceased to strike me how incongruous they looked picking their way arm in arm along a crowded sidewalk on a busy city street. To me they would only ever belong among the gentle hills and quiet, winding lanes of Upper Killington.

They had little time to be lonely or to mourn for their old way of life. Steve, who by then was a graduate student at the city's university, had a flat of his own in the same neighborhood, and was a frequent visitor. And he wasn't the only one. It seemed that wherever Mama built her nest, there, too, her children, although long since fledged and flown, would be irresistibly drawn. Soon after Mama and Dad moved, Sasha's husband landed a job in the same city, and the first tenants of the upstairs flat at 113 turned out not to be students but Sasha and her husband, their first baby now on the way. And within a year I, too, was living close by, having retaken my university entrance exams, passed with better grades (though still not good enough for medicine) and won a place at the university's dental school.

This time I was absolutely determined. I stuck at it through thick and thin, surprising Dad with my tenacity (which, of course, was the primary object of the exercise). Many was the time he expressed astonishment that I had not — or rather, not *yet;* he was always careful to add the rider — reverted to type and dropped out. But his cynicism only served to spur me on, each stinging reminder of his lack of faith in me prompting a further surge of resoluteness, and at the end of five years I graduated with honors, at the top of my class, a living, breathing monument to Stakhanovism.

I was a dentist now, with a white coat and a chairside manner and hands that smelled of mouthwash and cloves. I knew how to take pain away and repair broken smiles, to stitch up cuts and straighten crooked teeth, to stop hemorrhages and cure abscesses, to mend teeth whenever they could be mended and to extract them painlessly when they couldn't. At least now if I had to fill out a form which asked for my occupation I need never disgrace Mama by having to admit, with downcast eyes, to being nothing more than a humble housewife. As long as I was a dentist I could surround myself with the trappings of my profession, steep myself in its lore and define myself by its practice — and for someone with such a tenuous sense of her own worth and identity these were valuable assets indeed.

But however capable, knowledgeable and efficient I may have appeared in my professional capacity, in my heart I continued to limp along as before, hobbled by the deeply unfavorable opinion I held of myself. Those who knew me best at that time expressed amazement at how little confidence I had in myself. A chairside assistant with whom I worked closely in my first job as a dentist, and with whom I remained friends for many years, astutely nicknamed me Mea Culpa within a few weeks of our first meeting, and she never saw any reason to revoke that epithet. It was she who chided me for habitually making a doormat of myself, she who had grave misgivings about the man I was then living with, and she who, despite my heated denials, correctly diagnosed the cause of the gigantic, ugly bruises on my wrists, arms and thighs which began appearing not long after he moved in with me.

She implored me to leave him, but I was afraid. I had tried to end the relationship once before, but he had gotten drunk and beaten me savagely, blackening both my eyes, splitting my lip and breaking my jaw. My neighbors, on hearing my midnight screams and the sound of my body crashing down three flights of stairs, called the police, but they declined to intervene. Sorry, they said; it's a domestic quarrel; happens all the time; can't do a thing about it. Of course the next day remorse swept over my batterer along with his hangover. "It's because I love you so much," he said; "I can't live without you. I couldn't help myself." And I, Mea Culpa, graduate cum laude of the World's End school of self-hatred, believed my batterer, forgave him and looked for the fault in myself to explain his anger and violence.

In the end, thank God, his promiscuity saved me: he took a shine to another woman and slunk out of my life without a word, bequeathing me his hideous cache of pornographic magazines and a lingering fear of the male of the species.

"The Lord tempers the wind to the shorn lamb," Mama used to say when trying to console me or reassure me that troubled times would pass. Of course, she meant the quotation to be taken strictly metaphorically, and would have been horrified to think that she had contributed to the emergence of a spiritual streak in her daughter. Nevertheless it has always been a source of amazement to me how help often seems to turn up just when it is needed most.

Not long after the batterer disappeared an old friend whom I hadn't seen in a while called to tell me she was throwing a party, and wanted me to come. I hated parties and always had, but she was a good friend and I wanted to see her. She and I had shared a flat together while I was a dental student, and she had stayed on at the flat after I'd left and gone to London to start working as a dentist. I probably wouldn't know anyone else at the party, I thought, and I'd have to drive halfway across England on a bleak November night to get there, braving fog and black ice, too, very likely; but it would be fun to see her again, and besides, I'd promised to go and I couldn't back out.

When I got there it was exactly as I feared. I knew no one except the hostess, my old roommate, and she was far too busy to spend much time talking to me. I decided to stay a polite bare minimum of time and then quietly disappear, but just as I was easing my way upstairs to rescue my coat from under a mountain of others, someone tapped me very gently on the shoulder and said, "Are you the dentist?" I turned and found myself looking up at a tall man with the kindest and most beautiful blue eyes I had ever seen — and some of the worst teeth. His name, he said, was Len, and he'd been told by our hostess that I was a dentist. He wondered whether I could recommend a good dentist in London, which was where he lived. He hadn't been to the dentist in years, and needed someone to help sort out his accumulated dental troubles — "the rot of ages" was how he put it, and made me chortle with laughter. He was leaving England soon, he said, emigrating to Canada, and had to get his teeth sorted out before he left. I was surprised to feel a sharp twinge of regret when he mentioned his imminent departure, and I was suddenly acutely aware that something extremely significant — and something entirely outside my control — was happening.

I was right. Len did go to Canada, his dentition carefully delivered from the rot of ages by my own hand. But two weeks later he came back. He couldn't stand leaving me, he said; could we please get married? And so we did. Shorn lamb that I was, the soft May wind had come to warm me and to keep me safe from harm.

$\mathcal{C}$ h a p t e r
1 1

∽ There was a period of a few months after Len and I met and married when everything seemed set fair. We bought a little house in west London, acquired two sybaritic tabby cats (and shortly thereafter, two more), spent hours walking along the river Thames embankment or meandering gently through Kew Gardens. We were ecstatically happy together, and life had never looked better.

I saw more of Mama and Dad in those months, too, than I had since my years in dental school. Len and I visited them often at weekends, driving from London early on a Saturday morning and arriving at 113 — not unintentionally — just in time for lunch. Mama was a superb cook and she invariably prepared something splendid for us. Some houses — especially small houses — where lots of cooking goes on smell rancid and oniony, but theirs never did; it smelled of things cooked patiently, long and slow, and the air was always full of the light, flowery scent of herbs, drifting in from the little courtyard garden where they grew in obliging profusion. Even in the street outside one could often catch the sounds and smells of cooking: sizzling, basting, frying; heavy sauté pans being shaken back and forth on the stove, wooden spoons being tapped briskly against cast-iron cookware, and above it all the sound of Mama singing, absentmindedly and hopelessly out of tune, as she worked.

After lunch, if it wasn't raining, we'd sit in the garden and have coffee, talking and watching the bees blundering drunkenly from one flower to the next on the billowing clematis which clothed the courtyard walls. Mama would busy herself assembling what she laughingly called garnished buckets (*bouquets garnis*) for me to take back home to London — fat, fragrant little bundles of parsley, thyme and bay leaves all tied tightly together with string in a series of elaborate knots which would have done a sailor proud. She loved all things nautical, and knew her way around every clove hitch, half hitch and sheepshank in the book. Dad, who by then was seventy-seven, and entitled to a postprandial nap now and again, often quietly nodded off as we sat there — although he hated to admit as much, and had an uncanny knack of snapping back to life the second he felt anyone's inquiring gaze land on him. *"Dolce* fart *niente,"* he'd mumble. He never lost his sense of humor, even when he was half asleep.

In the world of art and style it is unusual for anyone (other, perhaps, than fashion designers) to live long enough to see their work enjoy a second coming, yet recent years had seen a resurgence of interest in the architecture of the twenties and thirties, and Dad's status as the father of British modernism had brought him renewed attention. He was increasingly being sought out by art historians, students of architecture and media people, something that he professed to loathe, but that he clearly found flattering nonetheless. Certainly Mama was immensely gratified by the renewed attention that was being paid to him. She worked on his speeches with him and accompanied him proudly on his lecture engagements, reveling in the accolades which were once again pouring in, just as they had more than forty years earlier, when she and Dad had first met.

It happened that Dad was due to give a lecture to a group of architectural students in London, and since he and Mama had not yet seen the house Len and I had bought they decided to break their journey and stay overnight with us after the lecture, returning home the next day. There was an exhibition at one of the London galleries which they very much wanted to see, too, and they planned to kill several birds with one stone. But in the event Mama, who had been feeling vaguely unwell for a few weeks before the lecture, decided at the last minute that she just couldn't face the trip, and Dad, unable to cancel the lecture at such short notice, came on his own.

When Len and I met him at the train at Paddington Station he was in a somber mood. This was the first time he'd made a public appearance without Mama at his side, and he felt her absence keenly. More than that, though, he was deeply perturbed at her uncharacteristic capitulation to the effects of what their doctor had dismissed as nothing more serious than a dose of the same itinerant stomach bug which had laid several of his patients low recently. It alarmed me, too: Mama was always so stoical; and although I made a point of being dismissive about it to Dad's face, I couldn't help wondering whether perhaps the old ghost of multiple sclerosis, dormant for so long, mightn't be on the prowl again in a new and bewildering disguise.

Dad delivered his lecture and, on Mama's insistence, stayed overnight with us as planned, rather than rushing straight home to her. The next morning I drove him to Paddington to catch his train, stopping on the way at the exhibition he and Mama had planned to see together. His heart wasn't in it; he couldn't even seem to summon the caustic and wickedly funny commentary which he usually delivered with oratorical ease whenever he was confronted with art or architecture of which he disapproved (which was often). Instead he spent a long time in the gallery's gift shop, silently browsing through books and gathering a generous selection of postcard reproductions of paintings to take home to Mama, and by the time he had paid for all his purchases, fumbled around with the change, lost his train ticket and found it again, we were getting perilously late for the train.

We reached the platform just in time. Guards were slamming the doors and yelling "All aboard!" — their voices and whistles echoing off the high, vaulted glass roof of the old station as Dad, no longer nearly as spry as he once was, hurried painfully slowly to the nearest car and clambered inside. The train had begun moving now, and I was running alongside it, shouting my good-byes to him, sending my love to Mama. "Here," he shouted back to me, throwing an envelope out of the window in my general direction before snapping the window shut and sinking gratefully into his seat. I ran after the envelope, which was now being blown along the platform in the wake of the departing train, and got my foot to it just as it was about to blow onto the track. Picking it up, I turned to wave one last time to Dad, but the train had rounded a bend in the track and disappeared from view.

Sitting alone on the empty platform I opened the envelope and inside found one of the postcards Dad had just bought from the gallery shop. It was a picture by the surrealist Giorgio De Chirico, an eerie, dreamlike scene, full of foreboding, with long, ominous shadows and inexplicable juxtapositions: an empty, desolate landscape with a tall brick chimney in the distance and another one beside it belching smoke. In the foreground stood a lone, empty railway freight car. The picture was titled *The Anguish of Departure*. I turned it over and on the back, in Dad's hasty, crabbed handwriting, was the sardonic message *Come and see us again before we die.*

When Dad arrived home Mama was up and dressed, although she admitted that she still felt very unwell. Steve had been with her more or less constantly since Dad left, keeping her company and cooking for her. But good cook though he was, he couldn't tempt her to eat much: she felt constantly nauseated, she said, and had painful stomach cramps. Steve called me that night. He was truly worried about Mama. She'd lost a lot of weight and had no appetite. He couldn't put his finger on it, but it just didn't look good to him. He knew I had some knowledge of medicine after all my years in dental school; what did I think? Could it be just a particularly nasty stomach bug that was taking its sweet time about leaving? Or was there more to it than met the eye? I didn't know: I hadn't seen her for several weeks, and every time I'd spoken to her on the phone she'd been dismissive about her symptoms, telling me it was just something transitory, that the doctor had seen her and he'd told her that it was absolutely nothing to worry about. I decided to visit and see for myself.

The following weekend Len and I drove down from London. Mama met us at the door, and the second I saw her I knew why my normally sanguine brother had begun to fret and worry. She was painfully thin; when I hugged her I had the strange feeling that her rib cage was made of wicker, and that she would break if I squeezed her. It was July, and hot, yet despite the layers of clothes she was wearing, she said she was cold. For all her cheerfulness it was painfully obvious that she was feeling awful. She'd cooked us a wonderful meal, as usual, but she herself hardly ate a morsel, and after lunch, when we adjourned to the garden for a cup of coffee, I could see that she was silently longing to flop into bed. There was an aura of tiredness about her, the sort of cobwebby, inexplicable tiredness which no amount of sleep can lift, and despite her obligatory red lipstick she looked like a wraith.

She went back to the doctor the following day. This time he must have realized that bromides and catchall diagnoses were not going to be adequate, for he examined her thoroughly and questioned her closely before announcing to her that he had felt a lump in her lower abdomen which he thought might be a kidney stone, and that he wanted her to see a urologist at once.

Kidney stones! Oh God, what a relief! Of course it'll mean an operation, but it's curable, damn it, *curable*! Even if they have to take your whole kidney, Mama, you won't need a transplant; people can do just fine with only one kidney. Steve and Dad, who had been to the doctor with her, immediately set about celebrating her kindly, calcareous lump, a lump which could have been so deadly serious but had turned out to be merely inconvenient. In less than an hour they downed half a bottle of Stolichnaya vodka, giggling like children and congratulating each other effusively, while Mama, her secret fears newly dispelled, slept like a baby in the bedroom next door.

The appointment with the urologist was scheduled for the morning of the following day, and before he lapsed into drunken incoherence, Steve had told me to call him in the early afternoon, by which time, he said, Mama would be home again and they would have some idea as to when the operation for the removal of her stones was likely to take place.

And so at two o'clock I called, and at two-thirty, and at three, and at three-thirty, and again and again and again, but no answer. Finally, at eight o'clock that night there was a busy signal. At last! They're home, and that's probably Mama calling me right now. Sure enough, just as I hung up the phone, it rang at my end. It was Dad. "Dad! Dad? What's going on? Where have you been? I've been so worried. How's Mama?" His voice was full of tears. "She is in

the hospital. She has had an emergency operation this afternoon. It is not kidney stones, it's colon cancer. You'd
better come now." And he hung up.

It was in Mama's nature to face reality squarely and un-
flinchingly, and the suddenness with which she had been
admitted for surgery had aroused her strong suspicions that
the urologist knew more than he was saying. His refusal to
specify exactly what procedure he anticipated would be
performed heightened her misgivings. "It's an exploratory
laparotomy, Mrs. Lubetkin," he had said, "and that's as far
as I can go at this stage. We shan't know until we get in there
how best to tackle the problem — nor even, for that matter,
precisely what the problem is."

"Well, what do you *think* it is?" Mama pressed him, but
he had continued to be cautious and noncommittal.

"It's impossible to say until we get a clear look," he
replied, "but there may very possibly be some sort of obstruction in the area of the large bowel —"

"What sort of obstruction?" Mama pounced on him.

"Possibly a polyp; maybe a fibroma —"

"I don't like things ending in '-oma,'" Mama
interjected, her linguist's ear homing in on the telltale
suffix, with its connotations of delinquent cells and
rampaging, cauliflowerish growth. The urologist smiled
indulgently.

"Many, many tumors are completely benign, you know,"
he said.

But when Mama came out of the anesthesia and discovered that she had been given a colostomy she knew at once that she was facing something a great deal more serious than any kidney stones or polyps, and the evasions and obliquities of the recovery room nursing staff only served to confirm her worst fears. "Your husband will be able to visit you tomorrow," they had said. "He's spoken to the doctors so he'll be able to answer all your questions. Now you must get some rest." And so began the systematic stripping away of what little autonomy Mama had left.

Mama knew she was dying. Sasha, Steve and I knew she was dying. But Dad would not hear of it, and punished any such talk with an outburst of anger the like of which none of us had seen since the bad old days at World's End. Unable to face the truth, he clung to the possibility of cure or remission, becoming furious with anyone — including Mama herself — who dared to even hint at a less optimistic prognosis. And having persuaded himself that she was not as ill as she looked, he reverted to his old boot camp philosophy of disease, oscillating between treating her illness as though it were an inconvenient and uncharacteristic display of self-indulgence on her part, and seeing it as a personal betrayal, a cruel and callous abandonment of him in his old age.

Two weeks after the operation Mama was still in the hospital, her weight dropping almost visibly. Her bones were now littered with cast-off cancers carelessly dropped by roaming groups of loutish tumor cells, and as she tried to get out of bed one morning she fell, fracturing her eggshell-thin femur in two places. She was transferred to an orthopedic ward where she took up her untimely membership among a dozen demented old ladies, who clattered their ill-fitting dentures like castanets and screamed at the ceiling. The doctors began to treat her palliatively, administering painkillers and sedatives in the hope that nature would take a compassionate view of her predicament and allow her to slip peacefully away. But they hadn't bargained on Dad. As the disease took its relentless course he turned his anger full blast onto the medical staff, accusing them of deliberately trying to poison her with narcotics, and insisting that she be given no medication whatever without his express permission. What's more, he said, the unpalatable hospital food was killing her: she couldn't eat it, and that was why she was losing so much weight. From now on, he decreed, we, her family, would cook and feed her every meal.

And we did. Sasha took on the task of organizing the roster of chefs and menus. Dad was to bring Mama her breakfast, since that required a minimum of skill to prepare; Sasha would bring lunch, and Steve supper. And at the weekends, when I drove down from London, I would bring two days' worth of dishes I'd prepared in my own kitchen. Having a specific, practical task to complete at set times each day in the cause of nourishing Mama was balm of Gilead for both Sasha and Dad, providing a sense of purpose and usefulness in the face of agonizing impotence and impending loss. Steve, too, got comfort from it, as he diligently assembled some of Mama's erstwhile favorite dishes using the recipes she'd painstakingly written out on index cards for him years earlier, when he'd left home. But I hated it with all my heart. I had been through a medical education; I had seen patients with colon cancer on the wards, shriveling up before my eyes, going crocus-yellow from obstructive jaundice as a result of the spread of cancer to their livers; I had heard them complaining of how nauseated they felt, how the very thought of food sickened them. Yet here I was participating in this cruel charade, the only benefit of which, as far as I could see, was to make us, the well, the healthy, the survivors, feel less helpless as Mama, sick, bedridden and without hope of recovery, drew inexorably closer to death.

Mama hated it too, and told me as much. Fearing that we might talk openly to her about her condition and her impending death, Dad guarded Mama jealously, dictating the times we could visit her and how long we could stay, and never allowing us to be in the room alone with her. One day when I was visiting her, however, Dad was called outside by one of the nursing staff, and Mama and I were left alone for a precious few minutes. "It won't be long now," she whispered to me. "I could go sooner if only you would let me stop eating. Surely you, with your medical background, know that?" But what could I do? Food was now the only officially approved channel for expressing love, and force-feeding Mama had become an act of faith, one almost Eucharistic in its symbolism. The thinner Mama got, the more determined Dad became to feed her, and the more sternly he commanded her to eat. Obedient to the end and, I suppose, hoping that if she hung on a little bit longer Dad might come to terms with the inevitable, Mama forced each glutinous, unbearable mouthful down, complimenting the various chefs as convincingly as she could before flopping back onto her pillows, her head spinning with nausea and ex-

haustion, her eyes closed in a silent prayer for there please
to be no pudding.

Yet through it all, despite the fact that she could no
longer even turn herself over in bed, Mama still struggled to
maintain her appearance for Dad's sake, getting the nurses
to comb her pathetically sparse hair and apply her scarlet
lipstick — now even more shrill, against the yellowed,
translucent skin of her sunken face. And clearly she read
her husband well, for his concern with her appearance remained just as prominent as ever. I remember arriving with
Dad for my visit one Sunday morning just as Mama was
buying the newspaper, carefully counting out the money
into the hand of the newspaper seller who went from ward
to ward. There was something so ineffably sad about her
purse, empty but for a little loose change; it was her last
connection to the other world, the world of shopping and
cars and busy Saturdays, the world she had left and would
never see again. Dad didn't want her to see the newspaper,
either, or at least not the magazine section. He had seen it
earlier, on the newsstand, and he knew that there was a photograph of a pretty young woman in a revealing swimsuit on
the cover. He snatched the newspaper from her hands, ignoring her protests. "But I've paid for it, Dad," she said
plaintively. It was no use: her last, small act of independence was summarily overruled, and although she was mys-
tified as to the reason why, she had neither the strength nor
the inclination to fight. On the way home after the visit I
asked him why he had confiscated the newspaper like that,
and he explained to me that the magazine carried a picture
on the cover which might make Mama give up all hope.
"When she sees how she herself once looked, and compares

it to what she has become," he said, "she will see no point in living."

He took photographs of her, too — yes, photographs, pictures of her lying there, helplessly tethered to her hospital bed by drips and catheters, the white bedclothes clinging to her emaciated body like a shroud. I can only guess how Mama felt about this: certainly I thought it was the most grotesque and macabre thing imaginable, and I know Sasha and Steve felt the same. In fact, Sasha, God bless her, sought out and destroyed the photographs. Unfortunately she couldn't find the negatives, and Dad, having looked high and low for the photographs and failing to find them, immediately had another set printed.

Mama was getting progressively weaker now, and it was harder and harder for her to bear the pain, but when she begged Dad to allow her to take the morphine which was offered by the doctors he berated her angrily for her lack of self-control. "These are not sweets!" he roared. "You cannot simply swallow them just as you please!" Incredibly, despite her pain, she fought fiercely back at her cancer, using the little oases of lucidity she won to talk to Dad about her death with a directness and urgency which pinned him down and brought him to tears, forcing him to confront the stark truth before him. She begged him to try to come closer to his children, to use whatever time was left to him after she'd gone — to tell us the story of his life, to explain himself to us, as she had so often promised us that one day he would do. And under her dogged and insistent pressure he swore to her that he would indeed do as she asked. His assurance seemed somehow to release her: her work was finished, she felt, and now she could go.

The last time I saw Mama was on my twenty-seventh birthday. It was spring, and I'd brought her the first daffodil to bloom from my new garden. Dad ushered me into her room and hovered at her bedside as I bent down for my last kiss. Every weary heartbeat seemed to jolt her wasted body, and she hardly had the strength to turn her head toward me. "I haven't been a good mother to you, darling," she whispered. "There were things I should have told you, but I couldn't . . ." But before I could protest that she had indeed been a wonderful mother, and that I loved her dearly and always would, Dad hustled me unceremoniously out of her room.

Late that night she went into a coma. We were all there next morning when Mama, brave, gentle, gray-eyed Mama, whose only real fear in life had been that she might outlive Dad, gave a small sigh. A single tear rolled down her cheek — and she was gone.

Dad took my lone daffodil from its vase on the table beside her bed and laid it lovingly on her chest. He kissed her feet, her face, her hands. And then, suddenly turning on the three of us with a wild anger, "You'll never know what you've lost!" he said.

The nurse who had sat with Mama during her last night pressed a piece of paper into my hand as we left the hospital that sad morning. "These are the last words your mother said," she told me. "She was very definite about it; she said them quite clearly; they must have meant something special to her." I looked at the paper. On it was written:

Remembering the past, in this dark house. It had to be a quotation, but it wasn't one I recognized, and try as I might, I couldn't find the source. It wasn't until years later, as I sat idling away an afternoon in the musty stack room of a university library in Boston, Massachusetts, that quite by accident I stumbled upon the poem "In This Dark House," by Edward Davison, from which those words were taken, and when I read it I knew that in her heart Mama had gone home to die. Home to World's End.

> *I shall come back to die*
> *From a far place at last,*
> *After my life's carouse*
> *In the old bed to lie*
> *Remembering the past*
> *In this dark house.*
>
> *Because of a clock's chime*
> *In the long waste of night*
> *I shall awake and wait*
> *At that calm, lonely time*
> *Each sound and smell and sight*
> *Mysterious and innate:*
>
> *Some shadows on the wall*
> *When curtains by the door*
> *Move in a draught of wind;*
> *Or else a light footfall*
> *In a near corridor;*
> *Even to feel the kind*

Caress of a cool hand
Smoothing the draggled hair
Back from my shrunken brow,
And strive to understand
The woman's presence there
And whence she came, and how.

What gust of wind that night
Will mutter her lost name
Through windows open wide,
And twist the flickering light
Of a sole candle's flame
Smoking from side to side,
Till the last spark it blows
Sets a moth's wings aflare
As the faint flame goes out?

Some distant door may close;
Perhaps a heavy chair
On bare floors dragged about
O'er the low ceiling sound,
And the thin twig of a tree
Knock on my window pane
Till all the night around
Is listening with me,
While like a noise of rain
Leaves rustle in the wind.

Then from the inner gloom
The scratching of a mouse

May echo down my mind
And sound around the room
In this dark house.
The vague scent of a flower,
Smelled then in that warm air
From gardens drifting in,
May slowly overpower
The vapid lavender,
Till feebly I begin
To count the scents I knew
And name them one by one,
And search the names for this.

Dreams will be swift and few
Ere that last night be done,
And gradual silences
In each long interim
Of halting time awake
All conscious sense confuse;
Shadows will grow more dim,
And sound and scent forsake
The dark, ere dawn ensues.

In the new morning then,
So fixed the stare and fast,
The calm, unseeing eye
Will never close again.

I shall come back at last
In this dark house to die.

$\mathcal{C}$hapter

1 2

֍ Life without Mama seemed to echo at every turn. She had been the linchpin of the family, the peacemaker, the mollifier, tirelessly trying to iron out our differences even as Dad was doing his utmost to deepen them, and despite the old enmities which still rumbled and churned beneath the careful cordiality of our dealings with one another, Mama's memory remained a potent unifying force, an icon to her fractious family. I visited Dad often in those first few months of Mama-lessness, taking him out shopping, helping him with his errands and cooking his favorite dishes for him according to the meticulous instructions on Mama's closely written recipe cards. There was a curious power in doing things the way Mama used to do them, and as the little kitchen at 113 filled with the evocative smell of her recipes coming together it seemed as though she, too, were there, her busy and capable ghost tasting this, stirring that, and singing, as always, sublimely out of tune.

That was the way I wanted to remember Mama, not as the

tortured skeleton she had become during her last months on earth. I wanted to think of her as she was in the "Young Communist" picture that hung in their bedroom: beautiful, confident, powerful; so serious yet so gentle; so blissfully unaware of the agony that awaited her. I had never seen death before. Oh, I had seen dozens of cadavers during the course of my training, but I had never watched helplessly, as if from behind a thick wall of glass, as a whole, vibrant, wonderful person, a person whom I loved dearly had staggered and stumbled, crawled and dragged herself in infinite pain toward absolute darkness. I remembered the way she looked on the morning she died, lying there with my one daffodil on her chest, her waxen face suddenly full of peace. I remembered the relief I felt, the sheer, exhausted relief, the first morning after she died when I awoke and realized that she was no longer alive, no longer inching her way through purgatory, laboring for each shallow breath, all alone in an aseptic, linoleum-lined barracks.

I was afraid that Mama's death might mark the start of Dad's decline; he was, after all, in his late seventies, and getting noticeably more arthritic. But no: if anything he seemed to have more energy, not less, and confounded the lot of us by turning into something of a roué, spending several evenings a week at the casino, drinking and gambling with gay abandon in the best Russian tradition, and shamelessly flirting with the pretty young women whom the casino — very astutely — employed as croupiers. His appetite for malt whiskey, his largesse and his staying power at the roulette table were such that the casino would send a limousine round to 113 to collect him, and to return him home, triumphantly drunk and sporting a glamorous croupier on each arm, in the early hours of the next morning.

He was more in demand than ever, too, on the architectural front. Requests for interviews and appearances came in thick and fast, and he visited us in London with increasing frequency, using our house as a pied-à-terre and often conducting his interviews, surrounded by cats and dusty houseplants, in our cramped and chaotic living room. I enjoyed spending time with him; he was the closest I could get to Mama now, and I knew she would have been pleased that he and I were seeing more of each other than we ever had in the past. Remembering how she had pleaded with Dad until her last hours of consciousness to use whatever time was left to him to make himself better known to his children, I often asked him whether he had yet begun to tackle the task of writing down the story of his life, but the answer was always facetious or dismissive — or both, as in "Bugger off" or "Mind your own bloody business." And, to be sure, what with the casino and the hectic round of speaking engagements, interviews and honorary degree presentations, there was precious little time left in his schedule for the task of recording his story — although I suspected that this was exactly as he wanted it, and began to doubt that he really had any intention at all of honoring the promise he had made to Mama.

So I was thoroughly chastened when, a year or so after Mama's death, Dad presented me with a thin sheaf of typewritten pages — the first installment, he proudly announced, of his memoirs. He had called the work "*Samizdat by Anarchitect*," but sadly the content did not live up to the promise of the title. There was nothing remotely subversive about it, as far as I could see: hurtful, yes, but not subversive. The *Samizdat* took the form of an open letter to Mama from Dad, the opening paragraphs of which amounted to a broad disclaimer, and set the tone for what was to follow:

Dearest Mama, [it read] *When you were admitted to the hospital I was suddenly and unexpectedly confronted with the problem of leisure looking ahead. You made me promise that I would use the time to record my past experiences for the benefit of the children. In the past when you and I worked together in closest collaboration, your hints and suggestions helped to cut my dross and drizzle down to size. But now I am on my own and I don't mind admitting that the burden of responsibility weighs heavily on me. Indeed, I have no store of wisdom at my disposal, no ready-made prescriptions or guidelines, and even if I had I doubt whether I would be able to communicate them to the children. In fact I think it would be futile even to try to discuss with them the values by which you and I chose to live.*

It is not that they are uniquely stupid or peculiarly insensitive, but they belong to a world which we discarded as fatuous and shallow, and consequently we severed as many links with it as we could. As a product of their time they live only for the moment, from day to day, seeking immediate satisfaction, preoccupied with approval and security, never even considering what purpose their actions serve. They are totally unable to generalize what is common between different events and sensations, and because of this they have no ability to interpret a seemingly disparate patchwork of ideas and transform it into a meaningful conjunction.

And so we dwell on different intellectual levels, and no wonder

*that communication with them is impossible, just as it would be
between two species related only by name, such as Donald Duck
and the duck-billed platypus. To view the past and the present as a
loose collection of fragments, without system, selection or organization — which is precisely what the children do — is to my mind
an unequivocal sign of intellectual degeneracy. In the circumstances I must agree with Bertrand Russell that the triviality of
the present generation makes it impossible to take an interest in
anything after one's own death.*

*What then? Shall I abandon the enterprise as altogether hope-
less? If it were not for the promise you extracted from me to stick
to this task through thick and thin I would indeed be tempted to
stop before I start. But one thing we both accepted, and that is that
the telling of my story does not imply a wholesale divulging of my
secrets. Most of these only you will ever know; I have solemnly
sworn never to repeat them to anyone else, and you well know the
reason why. I am of the opinion that secrets can be used as a key to
open the tradesmen's entrance of the mind, to negotiate a way
through the psychological maze, where all the answers are contained in the questions, and the questions arise out of preconceptions. You demanded that I tell the truth, the naked truth, since any
departure from the naked truth is supposedly "morally wrong." But
morals are as impermanent as so-called facts: they are but a func-
tion of human needs, and not absolute rules given once and forever,
never subject to interpretation, revision or criticism. All these speculations could be interpreted as a mere diversion from your injunc-
tion that I must tell only the bare, factual truth.*

*Yet what is truth? I suppose the easiest definition would be "a
correspondence of a statement with the facts." But what, for that
matter, are facts? Are they real happenings rescued from a bub-*

*bling stream of events, or are they simply the conflicting opinions
of alleged witnesses, distorted by stupidity, envy or wrath? The
nurse on your ward was convinced that Auschwitz was an island
in the Siberian archipelago. But even the most objective, unbiased
observer cannot be relied upon to sort out the relevant facts from
the turmoil of occurrences, since we constantly select the events
which fit our preconceptions. And this is the reason why I maintain that facts are simply a matter of opinion. . . .*

Dad's all-too-familiar scorn for his children, his long-
standing disdain for facts — now grown to encompass
morals, too, it seemed — and the suppleness of his interpretation of exactly what it was that Mama had so earnestly
begged him to do, made it abundantly clear to me that the
Samizdat — if it ever got finished at all — was not going to
shed any light on the mysteries of Dad's past. In fact, the
first few paragraphs alone seemed to me to be nothing more
than a tortuous rationalization of his decision to renege on
the promise he had made to Mama.

And indeed, except for this brief effort in the immediate
aftermath of Mama's death, Dad never returned with any
conviction to the task she had set him. He produced only a
couple of dozen pages in all, pages filled with stories of
childhood trips to Europe, reminiscences of school friends
and the pranks they had played on teachers, recollections
of the outbreak of the First World War. But for all their
vividness, these vignettes were a triumph of the escapolo-
gist's art. He conjured up pictures of Weimar Berlin, twenties Paris and imperial St. Petersburg which fairly glowed
with life, but he himself was conspicuously absent from

them, as though it were a travel guide, not a memoir, that he was writing. There was a randomness about it too: an almost deliberate disregard for chronology and continuity, and anecdotes were started invitingly only to be abandoned in mid-sentence, the scene, the setting and the subject abruptly changing for no reason, apparently, other than sheer caprice. Altogether it seemed to me to be a masterpiece of obfuscation, a monument to Dad's wizardry at saying a great deal whilst revealing next to nothing.

Even so, the memory of Mama on her deathbed entreating Dad to tell us his story continued to nag at me. If there was nothing else of significance in the *Samizdat* it certainly confirmed that the burden of complicity in Dad's vow of secrecy and silence had weighed unbearably heavily on Mama, and I felt I owed it to her to continue prodding Dad periodically. But it was no use: he remained as tight-lipped as ever, and as steadfast in his refusal to be drawn on the subject of his past. So I finally gave up asking; after all, even the most dedicated sleuth can get tired of being rudely brushed off, and I had been told that I was too stupid to understand too many times ever to want to hear it again.

Besides, time was at a premium for both of us these days: Dad was now at the center of a veritable social whirlwind, and I, too, was busier than I had ever been. Mama's death had brought me to a strange and ambivalent point in my life. For while my grief made me want to turn inward, go back, cling tenaciously to the past, warts and all, there was also a part of me that felt the need to change everything, to go in new directions, to take such firm control of my life that the reins could never again be snatched from my grasp. And

in this latter spirit I had taken the enormous step of opening my own solo dental practice, a venture which demanded
all my time and attention. I had done other, lesser things,
too, in my quest to reinvent myself: I'd stopped smoking,
taking a two-pack-a-day habit and tossing it unceremoniously overboard, the noxious weed that had sustained me
through the stations of Mama's cross suddenly having lost
much of its hold over me. Such is the curious way bereave-
ment rearranges one's life.

But tobacco is a wily and vengeful beast, and one not
disposed to look kindly on those who jilt him. Within three
months of my stopping smoking I had outgrown almost
every item in my wardrobe, and soon even the replace-
ments I'd bought — two sizes larger, to boot — were themselves too small. I had one pair of pants which fit, and I
wore them constantly, appropriating Len's sweaters to wear
with them in the forlorn hope that by swaddling myself in
something with sleeves which were far too long I might
somehow create the illusion that I was actually far smaller
than I appeared to be. In the end, when my one pair of
pants, reduced to gossamer fragility by repeated washing
and wearing, split with a resounding rip when I sat down, I
knew I had to do something about my weight.

I had never dieted before — but, then, I had never been
fat before. At five feet eight inches I had weighed around
one hundred and forty pounds for most of my adult life,
and had never consciously controlled my diet or watched
what I ate. But even so, somewhere along the line — encouraged, no doubt, by the emphasis Dad placed on physical attractiveness as a woman's most important asset —

the slow virus of body-hatred must have entered my system, and there it had sat, silently biding its time, just waiting for the right moment to stage its coup d'état.

And the time was now: suddenly all I could see when I looked in the mirror — and I tried at all costs to avoid doing so — was my massiveness, the behemoth I had become. I needed no support group, no Weight Watchers to overcome my inertia and get me started: to me it was a simple question of slicing my calorific intake to the point at which my over-upholstered body got the message and started to shape up. And it did. Almost at once my weight started to drop, and continued to do so at a hearteningly steady rate of a pound or two each week. I was soon able to squeeze into some of my old clothes again, and people started telling me how wonderful I looked, congratulating me, sneaking envious sidelong glances at me and asking me how I had done it. This was potent stuff. I had never realized before what a rich source of endorsement and approval mere weight loss could be. Encouraged, I threw myself with even greater enthusiasm into the fight to shed weight.

Within six months I was back to my old weight — but why stop there, I thought; one hundred and forty pounds is still on the solid side. Maybe I'll just take off another ten pounds or so, do the job properly, put a buffer between me and any possibility of gaining all that weight back again. There was something strangely comforting in finding that my original wardrobe was now too loose, and whereas I had greatly resented being compelled to buy myself larger and larger clothes as my weight increased, I felt none of that annoyance and resentment when it came to buying progressively smaller sizes. Before long the plaudits of my friends joined forces with the incessant chorus from bill-boards, movies and glamour magazines, and on some deep and inaccessible level in my psyche a fateful transaction took place: the self-loathing World's Ender shook hands with the new, reed-slim version of me and struck up a Faustian compact. Henceforth, the two declared, worth will be inversely proportional to weight, and self-esteem will be measured in pounds and ounces.

The result was devastatingly simple: the less I weighed, the better I felt about myself. There was a wild, exhilarating sense of freedom in the discovery that I could control my body in this way — a titanic, seductive sense of power such as I had never known before. My state of mind became absolutely contingent upon my weight: as long as my weight continued to drop I felt wonderful, but if it should happen to creep up, even by an aberrant pound or two, I would be utterly disconsolate, and would not rest until I had repaid my body's treachery in spades.

Soon, of course, as I reached the lower limits of what was physiologically healthy for a person of my height and frame, my body fought back, guarding its remaining stores of fat tenaciously and using some mysterious and exasperating technique of metabolic legerdemain to prevent the loss of another pound. But its victories were Pyrrhic: my body should have known me better. Raised as I had been on the principle that the more difficult something is, the more virtue there is in mastering it, I wasn't going to accept any compromise when it came to the question of subduing the flesh. By making progressively more drastic cuts in my food intake I was able to overcome my body's stubborn refusal to cooperate. I forced my weight downward once again, and within a year of my starting to diet my weight had fallen to under a hundred pounds. My periods had stopped entirely; I felt permanently cold no matter how warm it was outside or how many layers of clothes I wore; my face was the color of parchment and my hair was starting to fall out in large clumps. But no matter: if this was the price I had to pay for slender thighs and a size six dress, so be it. Besides, when I looked at myself in the mirror, I could still see room for improvement. Another ten pounds would do it, just to bring me down to eighty . . .

But no matter where I set the target it would be obsolete before I got there, and I would have to lower it further. In truth, there really was no target, no goal, no such thing, as far as I was concerned, as "too thin." The important thing was the process itself, the active losing of weight, and the heady sensation of absolute autonomy and control which I garnered from my ability to mold my body in this way. Indeed, the thought of just standing still, maintaining a constant weight, was frightening to me, since it represented a watershed, a fulcrum, a teetering, precarious balance only one small lapse away from the unbearable prospect of gaining weight. I needed constant reassurance that I had not gained weight. The bathroom scale, with its cold rubber platform, its portentous clang and its accusing Cyclops eye quite literally governed my life. I weighed myself incessantly, and each time I approached the scale I did so in a state of contrition and heartfelt prayer, as though I were standing trial before a hanging judge.

I was starving now, not just dieting, and my body was beginning to burn its own furniture — its muscles and viscera — in an effort to survive the siege that I had imposed on it.

Every cell in my body was screaming for food, but my entire sense of self-worth hung on my ability to ignore that desperate cry and continue to starve. And the hungrier I got, the more fearful of eating I became, sensing that if I conceded a single inch the ravening wolf inside me would steal several yards, and all would be lost. I thought of nothing but food, dreamed about food, spent hours browsing through foodstores and read cookbooks the way a zealot reads the Bible: nourishing the soul generously whilst sternly denying the flesh. And while I restricted my own food intake more and more rigorously, I sublimated my overwhelming hunger by inviting friends to dinner and cooking sumptuous meals for them, bullying them into stuffing themselves like Strasbourg geese while I sat before an empty plate, sipping Perrier and refusing to eat a single morsel.

I became an insufferable prig, too. The fact that I, by an iron effort of will, could override my own physiology in this way not only gave me an extraordinary sense of power and control over my body — and by extension, my life — but also made me feel, in some perverse and distorted way, superior to those who had no such power. People had long since ceased telling me I looked good — how could they tell me I looked good when the very sight of me made them wince with a mixture of pity and horror? Objectively I looked like a pile of coathangers, but objectivity was something I had lost long ago. I knew perfectly well that I had anorexia, but I did not see it as something pathological. On the contrary: I took great delight in my thinness and saw it as the embodiment of my strength and virtue. And if anyone had the temerity to tell me that they thought I had maybe gone a little far with the dieting I would simply smile with sphinxlike superciliousness, convinced beyond any shadow of doubt that their remarks had been motivated by pure jealousy.

Eventually anorexia pushed everything in my life aside. The preoccupation with food became so intense, and the effort required to resist eating became so constant and so enormous that there was precious little energy left for anything else. I could no longer concentrate on anything. It was impossible to read a book, for example: I would read a few lines but then my eyes would glaze over and I would not be able to remember what I had read or even find my place in the text. I was indescribably tired all the time, and numb with cold. I was light-headed, too, and rapidly becoming unfit to practice the exacting profession of dentistry. Almost overnight I seemed to lose all my confidence. The simplest procedure now caused me agonies of anxiety such as I hadn't suffered since my early days as an insecure dental student, and getting through a day's caseload of twenty or thirty patients required more of me than I, in my deathly ill state, could muster. My old feelings of being a fraud, an impostor, resurfaced with a vengeance — how could I call myself a dentist when a routine procedure could reduce me to a quivering wreck? When I wasn't dreaming about food I was dreaming that I had accidentally killed one of my patients or cut clean through their tongue with my drill. In the end there was no choice: I was simply too ill to continue, and less than three years after hanging out my shingle I closed the practice and sold it.

My sense of failure was overwhelming, and made even

worse by Dad's unbridled *Schadenfreude.* Although he had seen me frequently over the past two years and could not have failed to notice the dramatic changes that were taking place in my appearance, he never once remarked on how thin I looked, or how ill, probably hoping that if he ignored the problem studiously enough it might quietly pack its bags and disappear. And so to him there were no mitigating circumstances for my decision to close the practice: it was a case of quitting, pure and simple. Hadn't he always predicted that I didn't have it in me, that I wouldn't stick with it? He felt vindicated — nine years late, maybe, but vindicated, and there was nothing he liked better.

Poor Len, who had suffered every inch of the way alongside me, watching in helpless anguish as I starved, had encouraged and supported my decision to close the practice, hoping that at least it might remove a major source of worry from me, and thereby promote recovery. Neither he nor I had anticipated that my sense of failure would be so acute as to drive me even further into the slough of despond, but that's what happened. My profession had been my identity, and without it I had no means of defining myself, no sense of purpose whatever. Instead of receding, my anorexia grew to fill the void, becoming even more vital to me as a source — however perverse and illusory — of self-esteem. Starvation became my profession now, and I was terrifyingly good at it.

My descent into anorexia had been as swift and inexorable as though I had fallen down a slippery spiral staircase in the dark. Recovering from it, however, was not simply a matter of picking myself up and plodding stoically back upstairs toward the blessed light of day. For all its savage self-destructiveness there was a certain warped logic to anorexia: as far as I was concerned it was not a disease at all, but a way of coping with life, a means of achieving a sense of control, or managing the otherwise intolerable pressures to which I felt subject. Far from wanting to abandon it, I clung to it like a life jacket, guarding it jealously and resisting all pleas and exhortations to let go of it. And if that meant lying brazenly, pretending I'd been eating properly when in reality I'd been dieting more fiercely than ever whilst quietly spiriting my food into the trash bin, then so be it. The fact that anorexia, far from enabling me to survive, was actually leading me briskly down the path to my own extinction, troubled me little. I did not believe that I would die; I did, however, believe very earnestly in my body's prodigious ability to gain weight, and given the choice of the two fates I would infinitely have preferred the former.

I was therefore highly ambivalent about the whole concept of "getting better." While I very much wanted to stop feeling so ill, to get my energy and concentration back and to have a full, glossy head of hair again, I wanted these things to happen without me having to sacrifice my triumphantly skinny body, and I was not prepared to accept that I must trade in the one in order to obtain the others. And although eventually I did manage to reconcile myself· to the inevitability of relinquishing my hard-won thinness, it was a process that took several years — and frequent bouts of wretchedness and backsliding — to accomplish. It was something, too, which I was adamant I must do on my own. I wanted nothing to do with therapists or psychiatrists. To me the very idea of handing myself over to someone else, asking someone else to analyze my behavior, interpret my thoughts, tell me what was best for me, was not only bitterly reminiscent of the experience of my childhood, but also amounted to a surrender of the precious autonomy and control for which I had paid such a high price.

And so I designed my own cure. I read everything I could get my hands on concerning anorexia, from the most obscure medical journals and books on the subject to articles in pulp magazines, and in doing so I discovered to my amazement that the problems I had thought to be unique to me were actually rife among women. I put ads in the newspapers asking for other women with anorexia to write to me — and they did, in their dozens, these distant, emaciated soul sisters of mine, and I wrote back; and to and fro the letters went, each one a skinny hand held out to someone else alone and afraid of the dark.

Above all I turned to Len, who had always been convinced that although everything appeared to hinge on the question of my weight, there was a whole host of other, deeper questions at stake, and that even if I returned to a normal weight tomorrow, the fundamental problem would remain. He believed that if he could just keep me alive, surround me with love and unconditional support, I would eventually find the solution within myself and would no longer need to control my weight in order to feel like a whole and worthy person. And in the sincere hope of preventing my untimely death while the search was in progress, he presented me with not one but two Old English sheepdog puppies. Even seekers after the Truth need a little light relief — and furthermore it is quite impossible to feel useless and unneeded when there are two extravagantly affectionate puppies in one's care.

I knew at the outset that if I was ever going to pull myself out of anorexia I would first have to understand exactly how I had come to fall into it, and so began the long, slow task of rummaging through the past and trying to make sense of it, picking out the clues and the milestones and following the path they marked as it meandered all across England and down through the years, winding up neatly on the cool, flagstoned doorstep of World's End. Some of the clues were glaringly obvious: it was not surprising that in the wake of the grotesque ritual of forcing Mama to eat against her will I should have come to see food as such a potent symbol of autonomy, and the choice of whether or not to eat as a struggle for self-determination. But others were both less recent and less amenable to resolution. I pondered long and hard about Dad's role in my life, about the endless — and fruitless — effort I had expended from early childhood onward in trying to win his love and respect, and about the bitter sense of failure and worthlessness which had rushed in to fill the vacuum left by his indifference toward me. Might things have been different, I wondered, if I had been able to talk to him, if I had known him and understood him as Mama did? Hadn't she always said that if only we knew him as she did we'd understand him and forgive him? Maybe there was still time to undo the damage?

But he was in his mid-eighties by now, and unlikely to be any more receptive to the intrusions and inquisitions of his children than he had been some twenty-odd years earlier. And if Mama's deathbed entreaties hadn't persuaded him to tell us who he was I was quite sure my own belated pleading wouldn't. Besides, it was getting increasingly hard to pin him down these days. He was always off gallivanting somewhere or other, lecturing or being interviewed, and recently all his time had been taken up organizing a retrospective exhibition of his work which was traveling to several European cities. I only found out where he was when I got postcards from him. There was often no message to speak of on the back: sometimes just the letters *BL,* sometimes *Best wishes, BL.* The postcards were usually of places we had visited as a family on those grueling summer vacations long ago. Geneva was a favorite of his: he visited it at every opportunity and always sent me a postcard of the fountain, or of the statue of the philosopher Jean-Jacques Rousseau, beneath whose stern, magisterial gaze Sasha, Steve and I had once fed the park-tame pigeons and ducks with scraps of delicious Swiss baguette.

Sometimes the postcards evoked more somber memories, such as the one he sent me from Nantua, France, depicting the monument to the thousands of French Jews who were rounded up by the Vichy regime and deported to their deaths during World War Two. He knew how that monument had terrified me as a child, how I had had nightmares for weeks about that emaciated figure lying trapped beneath a huge block of rough-hewn granite. In the cramped and stifling darkness of the trailer, I had several times awoken in blind panic, flailing around wildly, trying to find my way out of the tight confinement of the bottom bunk, certain that the bunk above me, no more than a foot from my face, was the block of granite, and that I was buried alive. *For your album, if you have one. If not, time to start now. BL,* read the message on the back of the postcard. Positively verbose for Dad.

But Dad wasn't the only one who was on the move. There were strong rumors afoot at Len's company that he was about to be transferred to the United States for a three-year stint, a move which both of us were eager to make. The time was ripe for change: I was starting to recover, slowly but surely, from my anorexia; the job Len would be doing was one he very much coveted; we would be based in Boston, a city we both loved; and anyway, our little west London house was now far too small for us, what with the two enormous sheepdogs and the four cats. It seemed to us from every point of view that this was an opportunity that we should grab with both hands, and when the offer was confirmed that's just what we did.

The move put the final nail in anorexia's coffin, just as we had hoped it might. Away from my family, in a completely new environment, separated by sheer distance from the places and people I had known during my hungry years, unknown and therefore unencumbered by the expectations of others, it was possible for me to begin building an identity of my own at last. And as that sense of independence grew, so the need I felt to control my weight subsided and finally disappeared altogether.

We had been living in Boston for two years when Dad decided he would come and visit us. It was the only visit he ever made to us there: the transatlantic flight and the accompanying trials and tribulations at either end were a tremendous strain on an arthritic old man with congestive cardiac failure, whose various medications made him a slave to his own bladder, and he wouldn't have contemplated making the trip at all if he hadn't been invited to lecture in New York, all expenses paid. He stayed with us for a couple of days before flying on to New York, and while he was with us I tried unsuccessfully to broach the subject of his past, asking if he'd written any more of his memoirs for us. I did so more in deference to Mama's memory than out of any real hope that he might at last open up and confide in me, and that was just as well, for his answer was characteristically abrupt and to the point. "No," he said, "I don't write for idiots."

I went with him to the airport to get him safely on his flight to New York. I had offered to drive him there, or to fly with him and help him get to his destination at the other end, but he wouldn't hear of it. He was being met at New York, he said, and would be well taken care of until it was time for him to fly back to England. When we got to the check-in he couldn't seem to find his ticket. We went through his pockets together — what volumes of stuff he always seemed to carry: packets of Life Savers, handkerchiefs, bundles of banknotes of all sorts of denominations and nationalities, a similarly eclectic mixture of loose change, envelopes, letters — ah! there was his ticket, hidden among the notes for his lecture. He undid his attaché case and started fumbling around with it, and the next thing I knew the whole thing fell onto the polished floor of the airport terminal, upside down, of course, cheerfully disgorging its contents like a cornucopia. I was still frantically scrambling around, trying to catch the last drifting sheets of paper, when his flight was called. "Come on, come on!" he urged me impatiently, and he began shuffling toward the gate, cane in one hand, open attaché case in the other, looking as though it might spew forth its contents again at any moment. He looked so disorganized, so small, so much in need of Mama that I couldn't help starting to cry, much as I knew he would hate it. We were at the gate now, and people were pushing past us on either side. "Good-bye, chap," he said — we were all "chap," regardless of age, sex or circumstances — and turned to go.

But suddenly he turned back, and fumbled for a moment with the ticket envelope. "Here," he said, handing me a tiny, faded photograph of a long-haired little boy wearing a sailor suit and a voluminous straw hat. "I thought you might want this. It's me when I was four years old. Now bugger off." And he turned resolutely away and was swept with the tide down the tunnel to the plane.

I was absolutely enraptured with the little photograph Dad had given me, and not just with the image itself, appealing though it was, but with the gesture, also. I had never before seen a single picture from his past, and the fact that he had volunteered it rekindled my hope that he was at last going to honor his promise to Mama and reveal his story.

Sadly, though, my optimism proved unfounded. He continued to defend his past as vigilantly as ever, fobbing off my questions with increasing irritation, and finally declaring a moratorium on the subject, which, since we were separated by the Atlantic Ocean, was not at all difficult for him to enforce. I began to wish that he had never given me that photograph, and he himself must have rued the day he gave it to me, for it stirred my curiosity to fever pitch. Not since my childhood had I speculated so long and so wildly about the identity of the irascible stranger who was my father.

As I looked at the photograph, this tiny fragment of a past which, if Dad had his way, would soon be irretrievably lost, I began to search for clues, staring inquisitorially through a magnifying glass at the cherubic face beneath the floppy straw hat, as though perhaps if I looked long enough and hard enough those *kurrinny* eyes of mine might find something beyond the obvious. But all there was to see was a serene little boy in a sailor suit leaning nonchalantly against the arm of an ornate white chair.

But wait a minute. It was only half a chair. Why was only half the chair visible? And wasn't that the knee of a seated figure to the right of the little boy's elbow, just on the edge of the picture? Suddenly it became clear to me that the photograph of Dad as a little boy had been clipped from a larger picture.

Hoping that the detachment afforded by a letter might succeed where the intrusiveness of my telephone badgering had so resoundingly failed, I decided to ignore Dad's moratorium and write to him, asking him at least to explain

the history of the photograph, and to identify the other figure, whose knee hovered so intriguingly at the margin of
the picture. I wrote the letter a dozen times, trying to mod-
erate the tone, studiously expunging all traces of passion.
But insincerity had never been my forte, and I saw no reason to start practicing it now. I was his daughter, damn it;
the question of his past mattered to me. It had always mattered to me, but now it seemed to be looming larger every
day, and somehow I had to make him understand that as
long as his background remained a mystery a huge chunk
of my own identity would be missing too. Why should I
have to hide my longing to know him better?

And so, without circumspection, without economizing on
earnestness or corseting my feelings, without even stopping
to correct my spelling mistakes, I poured my heart out to
him, reminding him of the promise he had made to Mama
and begging him to reveal his story to me, now, while there
was still time. "Who is the figure seated to your right in the
little photograph you gave me, Dad?" I asked him. "Is that
your father? Why has he been cut off the photograph? Did
you not want me to have a picture of my grandfather? And
what about my grandmother? Who were they? Why did you
never tell me about them? Dad, I don't even know your real
name — who are you? And why don't you want me to know?
Why is it all such a secret?"

He replied by return, his letter full of sarcasm and cold
amusement:

*My dear child, your long and impassioned letter at hand.
What does one do in reply? Stand on one's head? As it is, it took*

me the whole day to wade through it, while all the time wiping the sweat from my brow and trying unsuccessfully to determine what I had done to you to provoke such an inquisition. I do not think that writing treatises and declarations is helpful. I fail to see the relevance of discovery of details of the past, which in any case is shrouded in the thick fog of forgetfulness and revolution, and can no longer be recalled. Please think about these things in a more reasonable mood, shaking off the excess melodrama as you proceed. Apart from anything else, there is an infinite variety of interpretations and speculations which could be applied to what Mama asked or meant or desired, and all of them amount to nothing more than gossip. Please discard your romantic view of events and use the puny organ which — I can only assume — occupies your cranium. Best wishes, BL.

PS: With your vivid imagination, you should write a book.

I never broached the subject with him again. I didn't get the chance. Shortly after his dismissive letter reached me he succumbed to a bout of pneumonia which kept him in the hospital for almost a month, and during that time he was in no state to write letters or talk to me on the phone. Rasputin-like, he recovered, and went home again — but not for long. His age had finally caught up with him, and even the fusillade of magic bullets — the diuretics and antibiotics, cardiac stimulants and antiarthritics — which the doctors caused to rain down daily upon his increasingly rickety frame could do no more than slow the pace of his decline, for his were the symptoms of a long life drawing naturally and ineluctably to a close.

He was only a few weeks away from his ninetieth birthday when pneumonia again took up residence in his weary
lungs. He returned to the hospital with an uncharacteristic
willingness, and sank easily into its regime as though com-
plaisance and meekness had always been cornerstones of
his personality. He looked tiny now, like a little featherless
bird fallen from the nest. When I came to visit him he
would turn his cloudy, tired eyes slowly toward me, certain
he knew me from somewhere, a long time ago, but unable
to place me or remember my name.

There had been a wedding at the city's old cathedral on
the afternoon that Dad died, and the bells were laughing
and shouting into the late October sky when I kissed him
for the last time and whispered "I love you" to the father
who couldn't hear me now, and never had.

There was no service at his funeral: no pallbearers, no
priests, no official mourners, no creeping cortege. Instead,
we filled the austere crematorium chapel with the sunny,
cascading sound of Chopin as Dad's lonely coffin slid
slowly away from us, adorned only with a bunch of brightly
colored anemones, the flowers Mama had loved most of all.
And with him, mysterious and triumphantly intact, went the
secrets of his past.

Or so I thought.

But a couple of days after the funeral Sasha revealed to
me that she knew Dad's real name, and had known for the
past thirty years.

Part Three

∾

Lost and Found

$\mathcal{C}$ h a p t e r

1 3

๑๏ For a split second after Sasha told me that she had known Dad's real name all along I was overwhelmed with feelings of anger and resentment. Why had he chosen to make Sasha privy to this most closely guarded secret, and not me? Why should she have been invited into the inner sanctum while I had been so resolutely excluded? And how could she have connived in this way, studiously hiding something so important from her own sister?

Sasha had anticipated my reaction: a Lubetkin childhood had left her no stranger to surges of primal jealousy. Indeed, whenever she and I had quarreled in the past jealousy had almost always been the spark, and mutual distrust the tinder. But now, gray-haired, middle-aged and with two grown-up sons of her own, she had seen enough discord and contentiousness to last several lifetimes. The shell game which Dad had instigated so long ago had impoverished all three of us. She wanted desperately to call a halt to it, to stamp it out forever. Dad was gone, and we were not sworn to continue playing in memory of him. It was time for us to live in peace with each other, for the rivalry to stop and sisterhood to start — and it was for this reason that she had decided to reveal to me the secret that she had kept all those years.

"I know what you're thinking, Lu," she said, "but believe me, Dad and I weren't in cahoots — far from it. If it had been up to him I would have known as little as you do. As it is, all I know is his real name — our real name — and that's the puny sum total of my knowledge. What's more, I only know that much because Mama told me."

"*Mama* told you?" I was amazed. After all, Mama had guarded Dad's secrets with the tenacity of Cerberus. Her loyalty to him had prevented her from so much as dropping hints, let alone deliberately imparting solid nuggets like this. "Why did she tell you? And how come you didn't tell me about this long ago?"

"Hold your horses. Just listen and I'll tell you everything I know. For a start, it wasn't a question of favoritism: Mama was scrupulously impartial, as you well know. She certainly wasn't in the habit of confiding in me. The revealing of Dad's name was something I forced on her, and she told me only with the greatest reluctance, swearing me to absolute secrecy as a precondition of telling me at all. A promise to Mama was not something I felt I could break, and that's why I've kept it to myself all these years, even though I often wished I could tell you: I remember how you were always so fascinated by the thought of him having another name. But we're orphans now, and I can't believe Mama would mind me breaking my vow of silence."

"What d'you mean, you 'forced' it on Mama? She was unforceable: I couldn't even get near the subject with her."

"Well, do you remember when I was nineteen I spent the summer at the Sorbonne in Paris? You were only eleven or twelve then, so maybe you've forgotten what happened, but at the Sorbonne I met a man I fell wildly in love with — real head over heels stuff. We wanted to get married there and then. He was Jewish, and from the name Lubetkin he was sure I was Jewish too. He was very traditional, and would never have considered marrying someone who wasn't Jewish. Of course I told him that Lubetkin wasn't our real name, and that Dad had acquired the name and identity papers of a dead Pole in order to get Polish citizenship and be allowed into Warsaw University — you know the story of how Dad got the name, don't you? Anyway, Yvon — that was his name — wasn't convinced, and since I desperately wanted to marry him the question of whether or not I was of Jewish extraction was of paramount importance to me. If I had been able to verify it while I was still in Paris, I think we would have eloped — I was that much in love with him, and I knew there was no chance that Dad and Mama would permit me to get married. But Mama persuaded me to come home and talk it all through, and it was when I got home, heartbroken at being separated from Yvon and desperate to go back to Paris to be with him, that I kept pestering Mama to tell me the truth about our real name. At first all she would say to me, over and over, was that Lubetkin wasn't our real name and that we were categorically not Jewish. Well, I knew that much already, and besides, it wasn't what I wanted to hear, so I just kept on pressing her, telling her I would go back to Paris and marry Yvon in secret, and in the end she broke down and told me.

And I mean "broke down." I remember it vividly. She was crying bitterly — she was betraying Dad, of course, and breaking the solemn promise she'd made that she would never reveal his name to us. I don't think I ever saw her more abjectly unhappy than she was then, and I was ashamed of how miserable I'd made her. I owed her the vow of silence she demanded of me. Anyhow, for what it's worth, Dad's real name was Nikolai Stepanovitch Makarov. He was the son of an admiral in the imperial Russian navy, one Admiral Stepan Makarov — very definitely not a Jew, incidentally! — who was killed at the Battle of Port Arthur in the Russo-Japanese War sometime at the beginning of the century. From what Mama told me, Admiral Makarov was a strict disciplinarian, and Dad hated him. Dad had an older brother who was an ensign in the navy aboard the Admiral's ship, and one night, as a punishment for some infraction, the Admiral made him stand, lashed to the mast, on deck all night in the depths of a frigid Gulf of Finland winter, dressed only in a thin nightshirt. Dad's brother — whom he adored, apparently, died of exposure as a result, and Dad never forgave his father for what he had done. That was why he shunned the name, and forbade Mama ever to mention it to any of us. And that was why he was only too glad to shed the Makarov name in Warsaw, and why he was only too happy to keep the assumed name and hand it on to us. End of story. Of course, after all that Sturm und Drang the thing with Yvon fizzled out not long after I came back from Paris. I was only nineteen, and once I got to college and met all sorts of new people I forgot all about him. Anyway, he certainly wouldn't have married me once he found out that we weren't Jewish. Mama never mentioned the business of Dad's name again, and I did my best to forget about it too, for my sake as well as hers: I've never enjoyed keeping secrets. I hope you understand why I did, though."

Of course I understood. It all made a great deal of sense to me now. I could well see that Dad might have been irreparably damaged by his authoritarian father, and by the loss of his beloved older brother. And then the rest of the family got wiped out by the Bolsheviks in the revolution of 1917 — no wonder Dad had set his face so firmly against the past. Maybe that's what Mama had meant when she pleaded his case to us, asserting that if only we knew Dad as she did, we might understand where his mercurial temper came from, and might find it easier to forgive him.

"By the way, Lu," Sasha interrupted my thoughts, "while we're on the subject of Dad and his mysteries, can you shed any light on this?" She was holding out her cupped hand to me, and in the palm lay a tiny white plastic teddy bear, no more than an inch tall. It was the sort of thing one might find as a free gift at the bottom of a cereal packet, or that a child might be given as a party favor.

"Where on earth did you find this?" I exclaimed. I hadn't seen that little bear in almost thirty years, but I recognized it at once as none other than my very own King Siphon, my childhood comfort and talisman, the magic bear which I had given into Dad's safekeeping all those years ago.

"Well," said Sasha, "that's the strangest thing. Dad kept

it in his wallet. Now you know what a cynical, unsentimental old bugger he was: he was the very last person one would ever have suspected of harboring superstitions or keeping mascots. But this little bear must have meant something special to him. He carried it everywhere. He was never without it."

It isn't every day one acquires a brand-new name, especially not one with such a dark and sensational ancestry. I had always imagined that the family closet might hold a number of old bones, but I hadn't expected to come upon the complete skeletons of a martyred uncle and a despotic grandfather, and being by nature inquisitive I wanted to know more about the cruel and overbearing Admiral.

I didn't have far to look. Hoping to get some general background on the Russo-Japanese War, I went first of all to the *Encyclopaedia Britannica,* and there, to my great surprise and delight, found mention of the Admiral himself. And what glowing mention, too: an internationally renowned naval tactician and author of a classical textbook on naval warfare, Makarov was a personal friend of Czar Nicholas II, and had been appointed by him to command the imperial fleet. The Admiral was also a prominent scientist and oceanographer with a string of inventions to his name, including the first cofferdam and the first icebreaker, *Ermak,* which he conceived, designed and captained on its maiden and several other pioneering voyages of discovery and exploration. There were even several geographical areas named after him in recognition of his oceanographic studies. My grandfather was obviously a force to be reckoned with.

Books on the Russo-Japanese War were replete with references to him — whole chapters in some of them, and photographs, too, over which I pored excitedly with a magnifying glass, trying to catch a glimpse of Dad in the grainy images of his father. But nowhere could I find any references to Makarov's authoritarianism. On the contrary, everything I read seemed to point to his having been universally loved and admired by his men. He was known as "Little Grandfather" among officers and ratings alike. Contemporary accounts described how the crew members of the Russian vessels under Makarov's command clambered on one another's shoulders, waving and shouting blessings at their "Little Grandfather" as he stood on the bridge of the flagship, *Petropavlovsk.*

Even his Japanese adversaries admired Makarov. Admiral Togo, commander of the Japanese fleet, regarded Makarov's book on naval warfare as his bible, and had committed it to memory — something the whole of Russia would soon come to regret, as the *Petropavlovsk*, hoist by Makarov's own tactical petard, was scuttled by a Japanese mine at the Battle of Port Arthur and went down, taking Makarov and all his men to their deaths. I even found descriptions of his funeral. The *Daily Telegraph* of London described the service held in St. Petersburg for Makarov and all those who died with him:

Within that vast temple the marine minister, the heads of staff, admirals and captains, the whole diplomatic corps, and the bowed figure of Madame Makarov are gathered together amid lugubri-

ous surroundings to offer the last tribute of respect to the heroic
dead who perished thousands of miles away.

Czar Nicholas II was there too, and Czarina Alexandra,
and Empress Marie, and all were in tears as the Mass was
said. Czar Nicholas's personal diary for that day refers to
"the sad and unspeakably mournful news" of the loss of his
friend Makarov.

Images of the dark, incense-filled cathedral, the ardent
choirs, the robed and bearded priests, the banks of gutter-
ing candles arrayed before ancient, somber icons; the
grieving czar and his family, and above all the lonely figure
of my grandmother, Madame Makarov, bowed and sobbing
— these images gripped me as powerfully as if I had been
there myself that melancholy day. Had Dad been at the funeral too? I wondered. Had he stood beside his widowed
mother, numbly mouthing prayers for the safe passage of
his father's soul while inwardly rejoicing that the Admiral
would never come home again from the sea? How old
would Dad have been then? Let's see, the Battle of Port
Arthur was in April 1904 — but that's odd: Dad was born
in late December 1901, so he can't have been any more
than two years old when his father died. How was it possible for a two-year-old child to have formed such an im-
placably hostile opinion of his father that the very mention
of his name became anathema to him for the rest of his
life? How could a two-year-old have known and understood the details of his older brother's tragic death, still
less have fostered such bitter feelings about it for so long?

No doubt about it: there was something about this story

which didn't quite add up. There must have been a great deal more to it than Mama had been prepared to divulge to Sasha. But there was no use brooding on it: the full story would never be known now. It had clearly been Dad's intention to wall off his past entirely, and if it hadn't been for that one moment of weakness on Mama's part long ago, then none of us would ever have known the little we now did. At least I finally knew what our real name was, and from what stock we sprang. Maybe I should let it go at that: after all, given the conflicting descriptions of Makarov's character it seemed that contradictions and inconsistencies ran in our family's blood. There was obviously a Janus gene on Dad's side. Perhaps it was best not to know any more.

But it's a very unusual skeleton which enjoys being incarcerated indefinitely in a closet, especially once the door has been pried open a crack. The Admiral was now a solid presence in my mind, and the more I thought about his life and death, the more intrigued I became about the discrepancies between Mama's version and the historical accounts, and the less inclined I was to leave the whole thing judiciously alone.

I searched the bibliographies of the books I had read on the Russo-Japanese War, looking for sources which might give me more biographical information about the Admiral. I called a naval college, hoping to find the name of a naval historian who might help. After all, Makarov was a very famous man: maybe there was a biography somewhere, a dusty, forgotten volume in the basement of some venerable institution half a world away. If there was, though, it would surely be in Russia, and probably in a military or naval library, which would be inaccessible to foreigners.

Over and over, I returned to the question of how Dad, a mere two years old, could even have remembered his father, let alone developed such a burning hatred for him. And it was as I was grappling with this mystery for the umpteenth time that I dimly remembered Dad mentioning something about his father in the brief memoir, *Samizdat*, which he had written shortly after Mama's death. I wasn't sure I even had those few typewritten sheets anymore; after all, we had moved house so many times since then, and so many things had been lost, broken or ruthlessly thrown away. But in the attic, amongst dozens of old letters and papers I had squirreled away in a box marked "Precious Things," I found Dad's *Samizdat,* and sitting on the floor, in a shaft of dusty late-afternoon sunshine, I read his words again.

Yes! Here it is:

But now, back to the central theme of the subject matter of this opus. I do not want to sacrifice information to entertainment as the BBC does, but since my audience is too stupid to analyze problems and is only interested in happenings and personalities, I am willy-nilly driven to display an assortment of vignettes, episodes, chit-chat and gossip. I am reduced to telling it as it was — "wie es war gewesen," as the German historian Otto Ranke put it. It would be morally wrong to do otherwise. But the fact is that "morals" in Greek simply means "habits." Now here is a happening that illustrates my meaning:

I believe it was in Rostov that I saw my first corpses. My father and I were visiting the family of a stern judge who was renowned for his unflinching rectitude and respectability. His rambling house was filled with icons, portraits of the Mother of God and the whole Imperial family. No wonder I was constantly admonished by my father to summon all my meager spiritual resources and be on my best behavior.

It was 1906, a time of unofficial patriotic troubles following the Japanese victory, and after the bestiality and excesses of the "patriots" the beflagged and festooned suburb was bare and unnaturally silent; the smell of fear and vodka was everywhere.

Somebody said that on the outskirts of the town butchered Jewish corpses were laid out by the roadside in front of their empty houses. They were easy targets for the mob, a sitting target, so to say, since they persisted, in the name of holy truth, in nailing Hebrew religious texts to the door frames of their houses. And now indeed their ageless feet were protruding from under their bloodstained prayer shawls in the light of a few flickering tallow candles.

But the howling mob, flags unfurled, fists swinging and national anthems welling up, having killed all the available Jews, were now looking for dissidents and free-thinkers whose houses were conspicuous by the absence of elaborate decorations and emblems of loyalty to the Tsar on that very day of some obscure court anniversary. As my father and I crouched in hiding in the cellar of the judge's house I could see through the window how the mob assaulted a student and savaged him so the blood seemed to gush from both his ears.

Then a strange thing happened. Along the broad, dusty road a black dot was approaching at great speed, growing in size and swaying from side to side, bouncing against the locked, beflagged gateways. A dog, who seemed to be dressed in a black fur coat, his white shirt hanging on all sides, was surging, strangely twisted by rabies, two amber lights gleaming in his eyes, his mouth foaming and frothing. The mob dispersed instantly, just vanished, leaving the bleeding student crawling with difficulty toward the judge's house. In my full view the judge went out, opened the gate and beckoned to him politely to enter and seek refuge.

When the hoodlums reassembled they resumed their search and clamored for the release of their victim. I was dumbfounded to hear that strait-laced luminary, that judge with all his calm and serenity, baldly lying, telling the mob that he had no idea where the student had gone.

There are experiences in life which seem barren, vapid or peripheral. There are others that have lasting significance. The one I have just described evoked a grave response in me, and the memory of it has stayed with me always, profoundly influencing my whole sense of values, and the course my life has taken.

Some years later, my father and I sat on a bench in the Alexandrovsky Park near the Troitsky Gate of the Kremlin, and talked about the recent death of the judge. "Don't ever forget the experience in the suburbs of Rostov," he said to me. "Think about the moral dilemma with which we were presented. There is a lesson for you." Of course I didn't take notes of precisely what my father said, but the gist of it I remember well:

"I am not a fanatical worshipper of truth or of conventional morals," he said. "Only hacks follow the rule book unquestioningly, forgetting that it is impossible to be virtuous whilst ignoring the consequences of one's decisions. As Immanuel Kant said, 'A decision which does not involve a value judgment is not a moral decision at all.' But the rejection of convention does not imply the acceptance of opportunism or the pursuit of selfish ends. Morality is a matter of individual conscience and it shifts responsibility for decisions fairly and squarely onto one's own shoulders. That is why freedom from external authority is only possible if we establish our own rigorous rules, a network of self-imposed limitations and voluntary constraints by which we choose to live."

I have never met anyone who would adhere so fanatically, persistently and fastidiously as my father did to these rigorous but freely-chosen rules of conduct. The impact of this discourse was never lost on me: it persisted throughout life.

Now how could Dad's father have died at the Battle of Port Arthur in 1904 and yet be alive and well at the home of a judge in Rostov in 1906? It wasn't that there could have been a confusion of dates in Dad's mind. He specifically says that the visit took place after the Russo-Japanese War. And then he talks about the homily his father gave him after the death of the judge several years later, by which time the unpredictable Admiral Makarov had been lying stiff and cold at the bottom of the Gulf of Pechili for who knows how long. What could it all mean? It just didn't ring true. I was beginning to feel that instead of knowing

more about Dad as a result of Sasha's revelation, I actually
knew even less than before. For if Dad's father really was
Admiral Stepan Makarov, then who was the man he referred to as his father, the man who sat on the bench with
him outside the Kremlin, the man who crouched in hiding
with him in the cellar of the Rostov judge's house, while
outside the vodka flowed and the pogrom raged?

There can be few things more harrowing than the process
of dismantling the home of one's parents after their deaths.
A child, no matter how old or gray-haired, is always a child
in the house of her parents, and the awful business of sift-
ing through their belongings, emptying closets and turning
out drawers seems to violate a most basic taboo.

The familiar smell which clings loyally to their empty
clothes, the cane propped against the arm of a favorite
chair, the reading glasses left lying on the open pages of an
unfinished book — there is an indescribable sadness in
these things which hurts somewhere deep in one's chest.
Even the most prosaic details of closing a parent's affairs
assume a terrible poignancy. For a while the mail keeps on
coming, blithely confident in the continued existence of
the addressee: the library sends a reminder about an over-
due book; the city peevishly demands payment of an old
parking ticket; a distant friend sends birthday greetings.
Banks must be written to, state agencies notified, pensions
stopped. Bit by bit, queasy with sorrow, a child must un-
ravel the fabric of her parents' lives.

No wonder none of us had any stomach for it. Even the

possibility that in clearing out 113 we might come across something which would help explain the mystery of Admiral Makarov was not enough to overcome our collective inertia. For several weeks after Dad's death 113 stood silent and untouched, everything left more or less as it had been the day the ambulance came to take him to the hospital for the last time. And who knows how much longer it might have remained so had not burglars, drawn by the widespread publicity surrounding Dad's death, and finding a conveniently private courtyard behind the dark and obviously unoccupied house, decided to make a start of the process of removing Dad's belongings without the assistance of his children. No doubt they expected a rich haul from the home of a man famous enough to command obituaries in all the national newspapers. If so, they must have been bitterly disappointed. Dad, never wealthy to begin with, had long since divested himself of anything remotely valuable, selling off what few treasures and antiques he had in order to support his prodigious latter-day gambling and carousing habit. Instead of an Aladdin's cave the burglars found a dusty and cluttered apartment, lined from floor to ceiling with groaning, overburdened bookshelves, every conceivable surface taken up with teetering piles of newspapers, books, old bills, unopened letters and yet more books. Even the bathroom was ankle-deep in old *New Yorkers*. In the basement they found a case of champagne — the Christmas gift of a grateful casino — and claimed it for their trouble, tarrying just long enough to consume two bottles of it on the premises. I hope it gave them an almighty hangover.

Be that as it may, the abortive burglary was a wake-up call, and the three of us knew that, like it or not, we must now deal with 113. Until that point, my only contribution had been to go through Dad's address book and write with the news of his death to those whose names appeared there — or, at least, to those whose names I could read. For despite having lived in England for the past sixty years, Dad had never really stopped thinking in Russian, and many of the entries and notes in the address book were written in a haphazard mixture of the two languages, often with smatterings of German and Polish thrown in for good measure, a vernacular all his own, full of quirks and puns and linguistic contortions which only someone truly multilingual — which I am not — could hope to decipher. Even Sasha, who took a degree in Russian and spoke it fluently, found it impossible to untangle some of the entries, crabbed as they were by the arthritis which had hampered him of late. Fortunately there were legible phone numbers for some of them: if all else failed I could always call, even if I had no idea whom I was calling. One such entry — a Mina or Mira Aaronson? — had what looked to me like a New York area code, and I made a note to try the number when I got back home to Boston.

But dealing with Dad's affairs at one remove like this, going through an alphabetical list and writing to people I had never met and probably never would — this was a job that demanded doggedness rather than fortitude. Sorting through his things was something else entirely. Reading old letters, crying over little treasures of Mama's which he had kept — at every turn there were reminders of the past, and I found myself reliving the emotional hunger of my childhood with an intensity undimmed by the passage of time. And although I felt strangely protective toward Dad's mess — the little knickknacks, the piles of books, the boxes full of newspaper clippings, torn-out *New Yorker* cartoons, opened packs of Life Savers — there was a part of me which would have been grateful to the burglars if they had emptied the house from top to bottom, thereby sparing the three of us the ordeal of having to do it ourselves.

It rapidly became clear to me that if I was going to get through it at all, I would have to work at breakneck speed, refusing myself the opportunity to dwell on the myriad evocative and painful details. I began frantically emptying shelves and cupboards, stuffing boxes indiscriminately, examining things cursorily and ruthlessly throwing out anything whose significance was not immediately apparent: a desperate triage carried out through tears and clenched teeth, as if in response to some looming ultimatum or disaster.

Sometimes Fate tiptoes discreetly at the margins of our lives, averting her eyes and keeping her distance. But sometimes she bustles around like an officious nanny, goading and chivvying, clumsily forcing the pace and pointedly shoving things under our noses so that even the most myopic amongst us are compelled to sit up and take notice. And it was she, I am sure, who led me to the old brown envelope at the back of Dad's bedroom closet; she who stayed my hand and roused my tired curiosity, and she who hovered invisibly there in the jangling quietness of the half-empty house, smiling and nodding to herself with smug satisfaction as I opened that envelope and gasped at what I found inside.

For there was the photograph of Dad in his straw hat and sailor suit — only this version was complete, and at Dad's elbow, sitting on the white chair, was a kindly looking, dark-haired man. On the back of the photograph, in faded Russian script, were the words "Roman and Berthold, 1906." There was a second photograph in the envelope, this one of a woman wearing a long white dress and carrying a parasol. She was smiling, and holding the hand of a little boy — unmistakably Dad — and on the back of the photograph, in the same spidery handwriting, was written "Fenya and Berthold, 1911." I was transfixed. The woman, Fenya, looked timelessly out at me from under her parasol, her dark features a curious, shifting amalgam of Sasha's and my own. That she was of a blood with us there could be no doubt at all, and I knew at once, and with a passionate and visceral certainty, that I was looking at a picture of our grandmother.

So this is Madame Makarov, I thought. But she looks so young: she can't be more than twenty-five or twenty-six at most. If the picture was taken in 1911, Dad would have been ten years old, and even if Dad was her first child she would have had to have married Admiral Makarov when she was only fifteen or sixteen. How could she possibly have given birth to another son before Dad, a son old enough to have been an ensign aboard his father's ship when Dad was only two years old? I suppose it is possible that Fenya was Makarov's second wife, and that the martyred naval ensign was her stepson, but that makes it all the more improbable that Dad, at the age of two, could have developed such an intense attachment to him or such a violent and enduring dislike of his father. Besides, how many fathers did he have? And who is Roman? Why would Dad have cut him off the photograph? What could he possibly have against him?

But there was something else in the envelope: a postcard, carrying Latvian stamps and postmarked Riga, Latvia, May 1940. It was addressed to Dad at his London architectural practice, and was written in English:

Dearest Berthold, I got a letter yesterday from your father in Warsaw. It is the second letter I have had from him recently, this time dated May 19, 1940. Your parents are healthy. They live in the old house still, but only in the kitchen because the other part of the house was bombed by the Nazis and burned down. Your father is astonished that he has heard nothing from you. Why do you not write to him? If it would make it easier for you please write to me and I will pass news to your parents. Surely you could write to me, your own cousin? You do remember you have a cousin Mira, don't you? Your father asked me to send food — butter and cheese. These things are not available now in Warsaw. Loving wishes, your cousin Mira.

It was an epiphany. If Dad's parents were alive in Poland in 1940 his family could not have been murdered by the Bolsheviks in 1917, and neither could Admiral Makarov have been his father. Among other things, that meant that Mama had lied to us; she had not simply withheld the truth, she had actively lied to us, feeding us a ver-

sion of events concocted by Dad for his own selfish, un-
knowable reasons. A cold, hard anger swept over me. It
was bad enough that Dad had chosen to lie to us; but the
fact that he had hidden behind Mama, got her to do his
dirty work for him, demanded that she deceive her own
children as proof of her loyalty to him, filled me with rage.
I was furious with Mama, too — Mama, who had set such
store by honesty and truthfulness — how could she have
allowed Dad to use her in this way?

On reflection, it was obvious that the anguish she had
displayed when she disclosed the Makarov story to Sasha
must have come not from remorse at betraying Dad's trust,
but from guilt and disgust at herself for lying so premedi-
tatedly to her own daughter. She must have prayed that we
would all simply accept the little we'd been told, and that
she would never be cornered into having to elaborate on
the original deception. How defiled she must have felt —
and it was surely her guilty conscience which had driven
her to extract the promise from Dad that he would reveal
all to us before he died.

But why? Why was it necessary for them to lie to us so
concertedly? What were they trying to hide? What had
happened to Dad's parents, living in a bombed-out house
in occupied Warsaw? And if Berthold Lubetkin was an assumed name, wasn't it strange that the name Berthold
should appear on the back of those photographs? And why
would Dad's own cousin call him Berthold if that wasn't his
real name?

His cousin! His cousin Mira! Suddenly I remembered
the illegible entry in the address book, the Mina or Mira
Aaronson with a New York number. Could she, by some

wild, impossible chance, be the same Mira who had written the postcard from Riga? Of course it couldn't, but what had I got to lose by trying?

The phone was ringing now, twice, three times — "Hullo?" said a voice at the other end. The voice was small and frail with age, but the Russian accent was as strong as the one which had clung to Dad all his life.

"Is this Mira?" I asked.

"Yes," said the voice, cautiously. "Who are you?"

"I am Louise Lubetkin, Berthold Lubetkin's youngest daughter. I — "

"Impossible!" Mira interrupted me. "Berthold has no children. Who are you?" She obviously didn't believe me, but I decided to plow ahead anyway.

"I'm calling from England. I don't know how long it is since you last saw my father, but I found your name in his address book, and I'm calling to tell you that he has died. Were you an old friend of his?"

"*Oy*," she said. And then again, "*Oy*. So sorry. He was my cousin. I have not seen him since five years ago."

"You're his *cousin!* He told us he had no living relatives — but you saw him five years ago?"

"Sure. He visited me here in New York."

"And you didn't know he had any children?"

"He told me he had no children. Said he was married for forty years, but they had no children. This he told me himself — why would he lie?" she asked rhetorically. Why indeed.

"Mira, can you tell me what Dad's real name was?" I asked.

"What you mean?"

"Well, Lubetkin wasn't his real name."

"Of course it was his name. Lubetkin. Just like me. I am Mira Aaronovna Lubetkin; he Berthold Romanovich Lubetkin. Why you ask such a question?"

"Not Makarov?" I continued.

"What Makarov?" she replied querulously. "No! Lubetkin. LUBETKIN. Berthold Lubetkin; only son of Roman and Fenya Lubetkin. Roman was my father Aaron's brother." And then, as if to quell once and for all any possibility of dissent, "Lubetkin," she said, once again. And that was that.

So there it was at last, the tiny, luminous nugget of truth that had lain buried all those years under a mountain of careful, interlocking lies. But still I hadn't got to the bottom of it all. If Dad was, and always had been, Berthold Lubetkin, why had he and Mama gone to such lengths to make us believe otherwise? What on earth was so terrible about being Berthold Lubetkin?

And then all at once it hit me like a punch in the solar plexus: the name, the postcard, the bombed-out house in occupied Warsaw.

"Mira, was Dad Jewish?"

"But of course!" she replied. "You didn't know? All of us Jewish — me, Berthold, my parents, Berthold's parents — whole family Jewish. All of us." I could hear her chuckling with incredulity at the sheer acreage of my ignorance.

"Our grandparents, then, Roman and Fenya Lubetkin. What happened to them?"

There was a sudden and absolute silence at the end of the line — and then Mira answered my question in a single word, a word uniquely eloquent in the rich and varied lexicon of human barbarity.

"Auschwitz," she said. And as she said that terrible word I swear I heard Mama's weary ghost, unburdened at last, heave a gentle, grateful sigh of relief.

$\mathcal{C}$ h a p t e r

1 4

૭૭ Mira Aaronovna Lubetkin was in her early seventies when she finally got permission to leave the Soviet Union, and came to live in the United States. As far as she knew, she had no living relatives. Some had died at the hands of the Nazis, some in Stalin's purges, and some — the lucky few — had died of natural causes. The only one whose fate she did not know was her first cousin Berthold Lubetkin, and soon after arriving in the United States she decided to try to find out what had become of him. Eventually she managed to track him down through the International Red Cross. She wrote to him and was overjoyed when she received a letter from him in reply. His wife had recently died, he said, and he was living alone for the first time in more than forty years. His marriage had been childless, but that had never bothered him while his beloved wife had been alive; it was only now that he was widowed and in his old age that he had begun to regret having had no children. He had enclosed a photograph of himself with the letter, a picture of a little old man with sadness lurking at the edges of his smile, his head entirely bald and his features crumpled and folded by age.

Mira hadn't seen Berthold since his student days at the University of Warsaw, and it was hard for her to reconcile the photograph she held in her hand with the image in her memory. He had always been such a firebrand, a handsome, brilliant young man who excelled, seemingly without effort, at everything he did, got bored easily and often found his way into mischief. His pranks were the stuff of family legend: she remembered the time Berthold had spirited a large white horse up five flights of stairs and left it in the apartment of a cantankerous neighbor. Of course his parents, Mira's Aunt Fenya and Uncle Roman, were heavily to blame for Berthold's willfulness and dilettantism: he was their only child, and they indulged him at every turn, never disciplining him with any conviction or consistency. He was thoroughly spoiled, that's what he was.

But when Berthold, at the age of sixteen, had started keeping company with communists, distributing Marxist tracts and helping to run an underground newspaper, Roman and Fenya were horrified. They had had to struggle hard to be accepted in the repressive and virulently anti-Semitic society of czarist Russia, and were among a handful of privileged, assimilated Jews who had managed to achieve a measure of wealth and prosperity. Now here was Berthold, who had enjoyed every advantage his parents' money could buy, referring contemptuously to them as "the bourgeoisie," and gleefully predicting the time when the dictatorship of the proletariat would arrive and sweep their ilk away forever. Roman and Fenya were well aware that they stood to lose everything they had under a communist regime, and were bitterly opposed to their son's emerging political philosophy. But what probably worried them more was the terrible danger Berthold was putting himself in. People were arrested and deported to Siberia on the slightest suspicion of disloyalty to the czar. If Berthold's communist sympathies were discovered, he would very likely be summarily shot.

Seeking to escape the revolution, and hoping at the same time to put a stop to Berthold's involvement with communism, Roman and Fenya had left St. Petersburg in 1917, just after the Bolsheviks seized power, and had gone to live in Warsaw. But it was no use: Berthold's commitment to communism — fueled, no doubt, by youthful resentment of parental authority — was total, and he soon sought out kindred spirits at the University of Warsaw, where he was enrolled as a student of architecture. The Polish government at that time was fiercely anti-communist, and did not take kindly to anyone — least of all Russian Jews — who preached Marxism and fomented revolution. Berthold was eventually arrested and briefly imprisoned for political agitation, and although Roman's money and influence rescued him, the incident was a watershed. Roman issued an ultimatum: if you continue to espouse this dangerous ideology, he warned Berthold, I will cease to look upon you as my son.

Berthold had left Warsaw soon after that, and the rift between him and his father had never really been mended. For several years Berthold had meandered here and there throughout Europe, never settling for long, exiled, Mira suspected, as much by his pride as by his political convictions. The last she had heard of him he had gone to England and had set up an architectural practice in London. It was there that she had tried in vain to contact him after receiving Roman's heartbreaking letters from Nazi-occupied Warsaw. She had never received a reply from Berthold, but that wasn't surprising, really; in the summer of 1940 she and her family had managed to escape from Latvia, and had fled to the interior of the Soviet Union, spending the war years in a remote area of the Urals. In peacetime or in war, no letter from the West would ever have reached her there: the censors would have made sure of that.

Of course she had always wondered whether Berthold had received the postcard she sent from Riga, if he had heard his father's last, desperate cries for help from behind the high wall of the Warsaw ghetto. But somehow she just could not bring herself to ask. He was an old man now, widowed and all alone; why reopen his wounds? What good would it do to resurrect the past? Besides, in her heart she felt sure that he had indeed written to his parents and tried to rescue them — but by the summer of 1940, of course, it was far, far too late.

It was a cold March day when I flew from Boston to New York to meet Mira for the first time. I arrived late: the Iranian cab driver, confused by my British accent, and none too familiar, either, with the geography of Brooklyn, drove me all the way to Brighton Beach before finally depositing

me at the address which Mira had given me. By this time
Mira had begun to worry, and had left her apartment to
take up a vigil on the sidewalk, where, bundled up like a
matrioshka, she paced anxiously back and forth, scrutiniz-
ing passersby for any sign of a family resemblance. By
some subliminal chemistry we knew each other at once,
and after an exultant hug, "*Nu,* come," she said, motioning
me toward the grim, faceless housing project behind her.

She lived on the tenth floor, down a long, narrow hallway
which seemed all the longer and narrower in the frigid, un-
steady light of the few fluorescent tubes that still worked.
The place reminded me unnervingly of a prison: floor after
floor of anonymous oubliettes, each scowling steel door
locked, bolted and barred against the world. But for all its
oppressiveness and menacing gloom, this place was home
to Mira in a way that her family's flat in St. Petersburg had
never been. She would rather take her chances, she said,
among the drug runners and teenage hoodlums who ruled
the stairwells and hallways of the project than be back in
the putrescent world of communist Russia, where walls
had ears, phones were invariably tapped and anti-Semi-
tism was almost a state religion.

Mira was as fascinated by Dad's duplicity as I was mor-
tified by it. She wanted to hear the Makarov story again
and again, and each time I told her she threw back her
head and roared with laughter. Neither could she get over
the fact that he had denied the existence of his own children — and so convincingly, too. It was hardly surprising
that she had been so incredulous when I introduced myself
to her as Berthold's youngest daughter. "Your father was a
wonderful liar," she reflected.

It must have caused Dad enormous consternation when Mira, whom he had assumed to be long dead, suddenly surfaced in New York. Having diligently kept his children from knowing anything about his family, he was now faced with the need to prevent his last surviving relative from knowing that he had any children, lest at some point our paths might cross and the truth emerge. And yet, with a gambler's passion for risk and a boldness born of decades of successful deceit, he had arranged to visit us both on the same trip, five years earlier, bidding me farewell in Boston and telling me he was going to New York to give a lecture on architecture, when in reality he was going to meet Mira. The old bugger. "There are no such things as facts," indeed. What would he have done if I had insisted on driving him there?

I had brought a spiral-bound notebook with me, full of the questions I wanted to ask Mira, each one with a space left beneath it for the answer, but in the event I hardly opened it, let alone took copious notes. The excitement of having found a living relative, someone who had known Dad as a child and could pin him down in history, someone who could vouch for his origins rather than speculating and theorizing — simply being there filled me with a curious sense of certainty. Unknowns and imponderables remained, to be sure, and probably always would, but the central mystery had crumbled. All my life I had wondered what lay in our family's past and who Dad really was. Now I knew, and when Mira showed me a photograph of her father's grave in the Jewish cemetery in St. Petersburg, with the Star of David and the name LUBETKIN carved on the polished black granite headstone, it seemed to me that Dad could have no secrets from me any longer. That simple, stark inscription was as eloquent and unambiguous a statement of identity as I was ever likely to come across, and I could hardly take my eyes off it.

My longing now was to know more about my murdered grandparents, poor Roman and Fenya, whose own son had handed Hitler a posthumous victory by ruthlessly effacing their memory. Every little scrap of information was enthralling to me — how they looked, where they lived, what they did — the smallest detail was priceless and the most trivial reminiscence a treasure. Mira had photographs, too — oh, what photographs! — pictures of Fenya as a young bride, smiling coquettishly, head on one side; pictures of Roman, prosperous in late middle age, dapper in his suit and silk tie, a watch chain draped from pocket to pocket across his expansive and eminently grandfatherly paunch; pictures of the family at their dacha outside Moscow, where, Mira revealed, Roman had hidden all their valuables at the outbreak of the revolution, hurriedly burying them at the bottom of the garden — and where, in all probability, they remain to this day, for no one had dared to go back and retrieve them.

So this was Fenya, whose face Dad saw reflected in mine that sad night so long ago, when, thinking I was asleep, he had sat on the edge of my bed, stroking my hair and crying silently in the moonlight. And this was Roman, the father of whom he had written so lovingly, and with such enormous respect, in the *Samizdat*.

"I'm sorry I can't remember more for you, dear cousin," Mira apologized. "It was all so long ago; my memory is full of holes." It was hard for her to grasp what an invaluable gift she had given me.

"Why did he lie to us, Mira?" I asked her. "Why did he murder Roman and Fenya all over again by hiding them from us and lying about his name?"

She shook her head and shrugged her shoulders with exaggerated slowness, her palms outstretched, her eyes wide. "Who knows?" she said, with the fatalism and acquired passivity of one who had lived most of her life with the unexplained shortages, institutionalized irrationalities and brutal injustices of Soviet communism. "Maybe he just wanted to protect you."

"Protect us from what, though?" I said.

"From the trouble that comes from being Jewish."

"I can't believe that was the reason, Mira; I mean, if he was so sensitive about the possibility of our being stigmatized socially on account of our Jewish ancestry, how come he cared so little about us being branded as the children of communists? After all, he made no secret of the fact that he and Mama were communists — card-carrying members of the British Communist Party, no less — and that was at the height of the Cold War, too. We were made pariahs at school because of their politics — and who knows what other tabs were being kept on the family. If protecting us was his goal, he made a lousy job of it."

She shrugged again. "Yes . . . yes," she said, absently. "But who can tell? Who can say what is in another's mind? There are some things you will just never know."

∞

It all boiled down to that name of his, that damned Jewish name: what a liability it must have seemed to him! From childhood onward being Berthold Lubetkin had been a source of inner conflict — and a source of conflict between him and his parents, too, for assimilated though they were, they never for one moment forgot the fact that they were Jewish, nor allowed their son to forget it either. Yet theirs was a curious, deracinated sort of Jewishness, a no-man's-land between the world of the *shtetl* which they had long since left behind and the world of mainstream Russian society, which beckoned invitingly, yet continued to hold them at arm's length. Seeking to ensure emancipation for their son, they enrolled him in exclusive schools where he was often the only Jew, and where, inevitably, he became the target of endless bullying and cruelty. And for what? he must have thought, bitterly. Lacking any religious conviction whatever, he came to see his Jewishness as nothing but a curse and a blight. The underground Communist Party, preaching the eradication of all religion and the establishment of a secular state with a single, homogeneous Soviet citizenship, seemed to have all the answers. Adrift, resentful of his own background and burning with youthful idealism, he was irresistibly drawn to the movement, and from that point on estrangement from his parents became a foregone conclusion.

Did he try to rescue his parents? I hope so. Maybe he tried and failed — who could have known, after all, as the Wehrmacht roared into Warsaw in September 1939, what unspeakable horrors lay in store for European Jewry? One thing is certain, though: he never forgave himself for the death of his parents. He hated himself for failing to save them, hated himself for surviving, for living through the war in the safety and serenity of rural England. And, having hated himself to capacity, he let his bitter self-loathing spill over to taint his children, those three dark-eyed, dark-haired echoes of himself, who reminded him daily of his parents and his past.

Somehow he had to find a way to deal with this terrible burden of guilt and self-hatred. The identity and fate of his parents must remain a profound secret, and to that end he must reinvent himself. Every thread connecting him to his past must be severed — most of all the fact of his Jewishness. The trouble was, of course, that he was already very well known in England by the name of Berthold Lubetkin, and much though he would have liked to, he couldn't simply shrug off the name and slide into a new one. Counting on Mama's absolute loyalty to him, he swore her to secrecy and made her the instrument and the mouthpiece of his deception. We were to be told that his family had all perished in the Russian Revolution, and that Berthold Lubetkin was not his real name at all. Together, they must have thought the story through from every angle, anticipating the questions we might ask and rehearsing the replies. What would happen, for example, when Steve noticed that his father's penis looked different from his own? How would they explain the fact that Dad was circumcised? They would tell Steve that Dad had been born in Tbilisi, in Georgia, where the climate was extremely hot and humid, and that all little boys born there were circumcised for reasons of hygiene. And what if the pressure to reveal Dad's name became overwhelming? What if Mama were cornered — as eventually, indeed, she was — and had to give us *something*? "It won't happen, if you are resolute," I could imagine Dad saying to her, "but if the worst ever comes to the worst, you will have to tell them that I am Nikolai Makarov, son of Admiral Stepan Makarov . . . "

Of course there were some things they could never have anticipated or rehearsed, and my encounter with the Nazi doctor in Bavaria was one of them. It must have chilled them to the bone, for there was I, paying the price for the Jewishness which, despite their most concerted efforts, refused to go away. Some lightning-quick thinking was called for — and some slavish obedience, too, on Mama's part. Better to affect indifference than to risk opening the floodgates of outrage.

No wonder he was such a believer in the capacity of the human psyche to distort facts and deceive itself: he was a virtuoso on both counts himself. Maybe he really did believe that by denying his children any knowledge of their Jewish background he was actually doing them a great service; perhaps that was just one of the rationalizations he used in order to convince himself of the rectitude and essential altruism of his decision. Certainly it seems to me that his mulish fidelity to the Soviet Union owed a great deal to the Soviet policy of denying the existence of a Jewish peoplehood and identity. Someone who desperately wanted to believe in the irrelevance of his own Jewishness would very likely find much to admire in a regime that insisted that the ninety thousand Jews butchered by the SS at Babi Yar were murdered not because they were Jews, but

because they were Soviet citizens. I remember one of the
most bitter quarrels we ever had was over the Soviet attitude toward Israel in the wake of the Six-Day War. Dad had
just delivered a philippic over the kitchen table at me, denouncing Zionism, declaring that Israel was a pawn of the
United States and part of an international conspiracy to
overthrow Soviet communism. Something flared up in me,
something wild and angry. After everything the Jews had
been through in World War Two, I thought, how could Dad
now be turning on the remnants of this poor people, denying them their right to a safe haven and branding them as
international conspirators? After all, he himself had
drummed into me how the Nazis — and before them the
czarist regime in Russia — had used conspiracy theories
to justify their persecution of the Jews. "Have you been
reading *The Protocols of the Elders of Zion,* Dad?" I asked
sarcastically. The response was predictably swift and emphatic: a clout in the face which blackened my eye within
minutes and left me looking uncannily like Moshe Dayan
— an irony which provided me with some small consolation over the ensuing week or two while the bruises faded.
Little did I know what a nerve I had touched, and how
close I had come to the wellspring of Dad's shame. For the
Six-Day War cannot have failed to remind him of an earlier, and even more heroic, battle for Jewish survival: the
Warsaw ghetto uprising, in which another Lubetkin, Dad's
cousin Zivia, had fought with the most extraordinary, su-
perhuman courage against impossible odds — and there
was yet another reason why Dad had to distance himself
from the name Lubetkin. How would his children have

looked upon the father who denied his own Jewishness and
sat out the war as an English gentleman farmer while his
young cousin, certain that she was going to die, smuggled
weapons through the sewers of Warsaw and hurled home-
made bombs at the advancing Nazi troops?

Oh yes, I am sure he was aware of the intellectual dishonesty of his own position, but this very awareness only
served to fuel the sense of self-hatred that permeated his
life and poisoned those close to him. People have often
asked the three of us why our father should have chosen to
abandon his flourishing career in architecture in favor of
becoming a reclusive farmer. Dad's version, of course, has
it that he made the decision as a result of his growing disil-
lusionment with the political climate in England at that
time, a climate in which the possibilities for architecture to
become an effective instrument for social change were
rapidly dwindling. But I suspect there was another, far less
ponderous — and far more personal — explanation. His
escape to the bucolic isolation of Upper Killington began
on the eve of the war, and his decision to stay there and to
bow out of public life entirely had a great deal more to do
with despair over the fate of his parents than with any
philosophical questions concerning the role of architecture
in society. I suspect also that his departure coincided with
a sudden and complete loss of confidence in himself, a crisis not unconnected to his need to recast his own identity,
and the feelings of shame and fraudulence which must inevitably have accompanied it.

Sasha vividly remembers the change that came over
Dad just after the war. The bitterness, the coldness, the

black moods and the savage anger started quite suddenly, she says, and she can still recall the acute sense of loss she felt when the doting, attentive father she had known was supplanted by this distant and unpredictable person. Powerless to understand the reasons behind it, Sasha attributed the change in Dad's behavior to the arrival of Andrew, and treated her young brother accordingly.

And how hard Andrew's death, so needless, so preventable, must have hit Dad, coming as it did right on top of the loss of his parents. One way or another, those early years at World's End were fraught with tragedy, and it is hardly surprising that Dad decided to withdraw completely from the public arena. Of course, isolating himself and his young family also made it easier for him to conceal his past and reinvent himself. In the sleepy, hermetic seclusion of Upper Killington he could control everything. Nothing his children read, saw or heard went unmonitored; no untoward influences could come to bear on them, no disturbing ripples from outside, no voices from the past. Only the chatter of swallows and skylarks could penetrate that perfect, timeless peace.

And yet it seems to me that for all the chicanery and obfuscation, all the lies and deceit, Dad could never quite bring himself to smother the truth entirely. As I look back on my childhood with the ineffable wisdom of hindsight, I can see many examples of revealingly Jewish things he said and did: the way he sometimes prefaced his remarks with an impatient "*Nu,*" for example; the way he jokingly referred to my chemistry lab-coat as a *kittel,* and his bathrobe as a *chalat;* the way he always said *"Naci na zdarovye"* (May you wear it in good health) when we got new clothes. In isolation these things appeared completely unremarkable — after all, we lived in a multilingual household, and were constantly hearing words and phrases in languages other than English. Even if we had recognized them as uniquely Jewish — and how could we, out there in the middle of nowhere, never having met anyone Jewish with whom to compare him? — it would still not have struck us as particularly odd. We would probably have assumed that these were phrases he had picked up from Jewish friends, habits of speech gleaned during his student days in Europe. Machinator that he was, though, I think he derived a sneaking pleasure from parading these things so brazenly in front of us and seeing how indifferent we were to them. Certainly it must have helped to reassure him that his identity camouflage was still working well, that he had succeeded in diluting his Jewishness to the point of imperceptibility, and that he had indeed become *Homo sovieticus,* generic citizen of the brave, new world.

But like the man who prays "Make me chaste, O Lord — but please, not yet," I think Dad secretly hoped that the truth would one day come out; he just didn't want to be around when it happened. So when Mama, whose conscience he had burdened so cruelly, insisted on her deathbed that he undo the wrong he had done her and come clean to us about his past, he was faced with a formidable problem. Somehow he had to buy himself some time, to transfer the onus for discovery squarely onto our shoul-

ders, to find a way of telling us without telling us — and
the *Samizdat,* cabalistic from beginning to end, allowed
him to do just that.

Confident that, lacking a few crucial pieces of information, we would fail to detect the deeper meaning in what he
had written for us, he was able to convince himself that
he had honored his promise to Mama. He had arrayed
the pieces of the puzzle invitingly before his children; it
wasn't his fault, was it, if they were too stupid to put those
pieces together and draw their own conclusions. How had
he put it in an opening paragraph?

*They are totally unable to generalize what is common between
different events and sensations, and because of this they have no
ability to interpret a seemingly disparate patchwork of ideas and
transform it into a meaningful conjunction.*

And indeed the *Samizdat* was full of clues, if only one
knew what one was looking for. Taken at face value, it was
nothing more than a series of unconnected snapshots of a
long and interesting life, but viewed through the prism of
Dad's Jewishness, the anecdotes took on a terrible significance: each one seemed to have an allegorical twist in the
tail. There was nothing arbitrary, either, about the places
and events he had selected for description — hadn't he always said that the data one collects depend upon the thesis
one is hoping to prove? And as if by way of a concession to
his purblind offspring, he had even included no fewer than
five direct mentions of Auschwitz. How could I have failed
to see it? That terrifying account of the pogrom in the out-

skirts of Rostov, with the butchered Jewish corpses wrapped in their prayer shawls, and Dad and his father hiding in the judge's cellar — why would they be hiding there, for heaven's sake, unless they were in mortal danger? No wonder Dad ended that passage with the statement:

> *There are experiences in life which seem barren, vapid or peripheral. There are others that have lasting significance. The one I have just described evoked a grave response in me, and the memory of it has stayed with me always, profoundly influencing my whole sense of values, and the course my life has taken.*

What he was saying, I now understood, was that he had learned very early how dangerous it was to be Jewish, how difficult and how painful. Although he and his father had survived the pogrom by hiding in the cellar, later on only he, far away at World's End, would survive: there would be no cellar, no kindly judge to save Roman and Fenya Lubetkin from the consequences of being Jewish.

Later in the *Samizdat* he describes a dog belonging to Zalesski, a friend of his from student days. The dog — a ferocious-looking creature with a face full of teeth and a growl befitting Cerberus himself — had been bought by Dad's friend for the purpose of guarding his property, and he looked every inch the part. However, unbeknown to Zalesski, the dog had been badly beaten in the past, and no longer had the stomach to stand and fight. The first time a stranger came to Zalesski's house the dog put his tail between his legs, bolted out of the house and was never seen again. *From Zalesski's dog,* Dad wrote, *I learned moral nihilism: that when survival is threatened, you run. To hell with duty.*

The trouble was, survival presented Dad with an insoluble dilemma. By hiding his Jewishness and denying his own identity he was in effect turning his back on his parents, abandoning them to their horrible fate, murdering them all over again. It's not surprising that he felt such kinship with Zalesski's dog, seeing himself as a coward and hating himself accordingly. But I believe that, unlike Zalesski's dog, Dad longed to stop running and come home. At the end of the *Samizdat,* he talks about the visit he and Mama made to Warsaw just after the war:

Warsaw resembled a crushed brick and lime pudding that had just been tipped out of the mold. The top was flat — some ten feet high — and only a few fragments protruded and signaled the buildings that were buried underneath. Gangs of youths were shoveling the rubble from the pavement and trying to clear the streets.

Walking in the direction of where I used to live, we found the area easy to identify by the remains of the Central Telephone Exchange. This huge ruin was entangled in a thousand torn and twisted wires. A single wire remained operational, and on it a solitary crow settled and was silent.

In this lunar landscape the only vertical fixture was part of the elevation of the very house in which I lived when I was studying at the Architectural Faculty. There was the familiar entrance above

*the workshop, and on the very top the same balcony where I used
to study descriptive geometry, under a large cornice supported by
two caryatids. How well I remembered their timeless smiles, that
serene confidence in permanence and continuity. They were still
dreaming dreams of eternity when the demolition brigades started
to batter at the remainder of the ruin.*

If Dad had really wanted to keep the tragedy of his past a
secret for all time, wouldn't the safest thing have been to
have torn cousin Mira's postcard into a thousand pieces
and burned it, rather than keeping it carefully for fifty
years?

And the story of Admiral Makarov, so transparent, so
full of glaring inconsistencies, so easily investigated — if
he had really wanted to bury his identity, he would surely
have told Mama to tell us — or could have told us himself,
for that matter — that he was John Doe, Ivan Ivanovich,
son of some anonymous, faceless nobody from Vladivostok,
or somewhere equally remote. Why risk piquing our
curiosity by telling us he was the son of someone internationally famous, someone whose birth, life and death were
recorded in the history books for all to see?

And the photograph, the little photograph he gave me
shortly before he died, with Roman almost cut off the
picture — but not *quite* — what else was that but an invitation to look further? What else was it but a metaphor, an
eloquent symbol of the rift between him and his father,
between him and his own identity?

I believe Dad wanted to be found, and I think he knew
that one day I would find him. He didn't call me *kurrinny*

eyes for nothing. But what he could never have anticipated was that in the process of searching for him I would also find myself — not only among the landmarks of my childhood at World's End, nor even in finally making my peace with him, but perhaps most of all in proudly taking my place among a people, a people with four thousand years of history behind them, a people of whom he, Roman and Fenya were but three representatives.

On a snowy January afternoon not quite four years after Dad's death, I appeared before a rabbinical court in Boston and, having satisfied the three presiding rabbis that I knew exactly what I was letting myself in for, was formally pronounced a Jew.

$\mathcal{C}$ h a p t e r

1 5

෨෨ I'm heading out of London in a rented car, taking the M-4 west, with the afternoon sun in my eyes. It's been a while since I drove on the left, and I had forgotten how fast people drive in England. What with that and the unfamiliar car, I'm more than a little nervous. Still, I'm going through with it: I have to fly back to Boston tomorrow morning so this is my only chance. I won't be back here for a long, long time — and anyway, it's the fourth anniversary of Dad's death today. I owe him this visit.

God, how quickly things change around here. Last time I passed this way these were open fields. Now there's a host of new buildings — offices, offices, offices; Reading bleeding into Newbury, Newbury into Swindon, and the motorway running through the middle like a zipper. Dad would have taken a grim pleasure in the ugliness of it all. "As men think, so they build, and this is the architecture of psychosis." That's what he would say if he were here, sitting next to me in this strange, looking-glass car, bowling across England, back to the place he called Happy Killington, the place he loved most of all.

It's been eleven years since I left England for the United States, and now I feel like an outsider here — but then that's what happens to us rootless cosmopolitans, isn't it, Dad? Even so, I'm attached to it. The oddest things can tug at me: the landscape, mainly, with those hedgerows crisscrossing it, the greenness of England, and the birdsongs. What things did you carry with you, Dad, on your travels? What things tugged at your heartstrings? Chopin did, that's for sure; and those caryatids on the balcony of your father's house in Warsaw — oh, I know it wasn't just your student lodgings, Dad, despite the impression you gave to that effect in the *Samizdat.* How do I know? I went to the New York Public Library and looked through the archives. They've got all the Warsaw telephone books there from the turn of the century onward. Your father's name is in there, Roman Lubetkin, #93 Aleja Jerozolimska — Jerusalem Avenue: how appropriate! He's in there every year from 1917 until 1940 — and then he just disappears. I found a photograph of the Aleja Jerozolimska in a book on Warsaw's architecture. Armies of caryatids smiling calmly from upstairs balconies. You went back there after the war to try to find your parents, didn't you, Dad, and all you found was the ruined house.

We must be getting close now — there's the sign for the Bristol turnoff, and the directions Sasha gave me say I have to take the next exit after that, and go north. It's so long since I've been there — I haven't been back since that awful night when you hit me and I walked out; it must be nearly thirty years ago. Do you remember that, Dad? Do you remember how I came back from Germany with my hand stitched up like Frankenstein and my nipples broken open and abscessed? The Nazi doctor knew, didn't he, Dad? He was no fool. He could tell a Jew a mile away, even a *mischling* like me. Right every time. I never told you this, Dad, but the day after it happened, Sabine and I went to Salzburg for the day, on a bus from Munich. I was feeling lousy, and quickly dropped off to sleep in spite of the rowdy group of young men — soldiers, they were, in their uniforms — sitting at the back of the bus. The bus was due to make one stop on the way to Salzburg: at Berchtesgaden, in the Bavarian Alps — Hitler's mountain retreat. But it wasn't the bus's stopping that woke me up; it was the sound of male voices, singing triumphantly. They were singing the *Horst Wessel* song, Dad, and when they finished everyone in the bus applauded.

Here we are, this is our turnoff. Oh, how nice it is to get off the motorway and go a little slower. Nice to get the sun out of my eyes too. It'll be setting soon; the sky's already blushing. Look at those limestone walls! I'd forgotten just how lovely it is around here. Desolate, but lovely. Not far to go now. This is the way you used to drive me to school, Dad — and look! There's the Spine!

> *Why do your eyes shine?*
> *Because I see the Spine,*
> *Right along the line,*
> *Discovered by Doctor Klein*

And his girlfriend, Gertrude Stein.
They came from Heidelberg on Rhine
In the year nineteen hundred and thirty-nine,
Bringing their pet porcupine . . .

See, Dad, I still remember it, even after all these years! I can't remember what I ate for breakfast today, but I can still remember the Spine.

Here's Starvenhall — at least I think so; the old barn's gone now, but I can still see where it once stood. I'll leave the car here, I think, and walk down to the valley like you and Mama did that first time you ever set eyes on World's End.

And there it is, the old house, still pretty much the same, you'll be glad to hear — although they've cut down the beech tree that was Mama's pride and joy, the copper beech over by the barn, with the smooth silvery gray bark which looked like elephant's skin. I don't think you'd like the bright red Porsche in the driveway, either, nor the satellite dish in the front garden. Of course, it's not the back of beyond anymore, not now that there's the motorway and all those high-speed trains. I wonder who lives here now? Londoners, I expect, down for the weekend. Better be careful they don't see me, I suppose, although I don't think they will: the sun's almost gone now — just look at that sky! — and they won't notice me out here in the orchard among the trees.

Well, here you are, Dad. I've come to see you because I know your spirit is here. Mama's, too. I'll always be able to find you both here. Look: I've brought you something. Recognize it? It's King Siphon, Dad, remember? I'm going to bury him right here under this apple tree for you, among the little daffodils. No: he's yours, Dad. I mean it. You need him more than I do; I think you always did.